"*For Conscience' Sake* is a good reminder of the struggles three generations went through in responding to the question of war and the draft. We need these stories from history to encourage us in our day and to call us to faithfulness in following Christ and his way of peace. The book reminds us that the way of peace is always costly. It shows that each generation must decide what faithfulness to Christ means and must bear the cost of such a decision."

—John M. Drescher, Author
Why I Am a Conscientious Objector

"Solomon Stucky's short novel, *For Conscience' Sake*, tells a three-generation Mennonite story of changing pacifist experiences in three twentieth-century American wars—World War I, World War II, and Vietnam. It is a story of people rooted in community and in the soil, and how these roots are tested, torn, and reclaimed. Grandfather plowed with horses; father plowed with steel-lugged tractor; and son, raised away from the home community, returns as a farmhand to plow in an air-conditioned cab on a huge machine. How can the younger generation, alienated from a heritage of faith and land, be moved by the biblical nonresistant values of the ancestors?

The author locates the story in a specific community—the

Swiss-Volhynian Mennonites of Moundridge, Kansas. The events of the narrative are often fictionalized accounts of things that actually happened. But the overriding message is universal."

—James C. Juhnke
Professor of History
Bethel College (Kansas)

"*For Conscience' Sake* is an absorbing book. From the harassment of conscientious objectors in army camps to the excitement of anti-war demonstrations during the 1960s, we feel anger, anguish, and perplexity as we empathize with the plight of the protagonist in each of the three parts of the novel. The book as a whole culminates with the story of Michael, a typical college student of the sixties who comes from a Mennonite background and rediscovers his roots. The story of how he makes up his mind, how his grandfather in Part One and his father in Part Two shaped his life and his decision, is told with literary skill and sensitivity.

"Because he is portraying the lives of fallible human beings, more or less faithful to their heritage of nonresistance, the author gives us a story which is at once more interesting and more relevant to our fractured lives than a theological tract."

—Maynard Kaufman
Department of Religion
Western Michigan University

For CONSCIENCE' SAKE

Solomon Stucky

HERALD PRESS
Kitchener, Ontario
Scottdale, Pennsylvania
1983

Canadian Cataloguing in Publication Data

Stucky, Solomon, 1923-
    For conscience' sake

ISBN 0-8361-3333-1

I. Title.

PS8587.T82F67   C813'.54   C83-098283-3
PR9199.3.S865F67

FOR CONSCIENCE' SAKE
Copyright © 1983 by Herald Press, Kitchener, Ont. N2G 4M5
    Published simultaneously in the United States by
    Herald Press, Scottdale, Pa. 15683
Library of Congress Catalog Card Number: 83-80452
International Standard Book Number: 0-8361-3333-1
Printed in the United States of America
Design: Alice B. Shetler/Cover Art: James Converse

83 84 85 86 87 88 10 9 8 7 6 5 4 3 2 1

Contents

Preface

Mennonites are the heirs of the radical sixteenth-century reformers called Anabaptists. They were radical because they believed that to take Christ seriously called for the total abandonment of all social and political structures, value systems, and institutions. They believed they must abandon the world order and begin to live in the kingdom of God, the rules of which were outlined in the Sermon on the Mount with its emphasis on pacifism.

The movement started in Switzerland where its adherents were horribly persecuted. Most of them fled across the border into France and South Germany. Forbidden to proselytize, they retreated from the world and taught their faith to their children. Throughout the eighteenth and early nineteenth centuries there was a steady stream of emigration of these Swiss Mennonites to North America. They settled first in Pennsylvania and then began to establish communities in other states and in Ontario.

Soon after the birth of the movement in Switzerland, it spread to the Netherlands where, under Spanish domination, Protestants and Anabaptists alike fell victim to the Inquisition. The Dutch Anabaptists were unified through the writings of an exiled leader named Menno Simons, and were called Mennists, and later, Mennonites. The name was also applied to the Swiss Anabaptists when they migrated to North America.

In the early days of the movement many of the Dutch Mennonites fled to Poland where they settled on the Vistula Delta. Throughout the next two centuries the area experienced increasing domination by Prussia and was eventually confiscated by Prussia. The new rulers were not sympathetic to pacifism and, beginning in the 1780s, many of the Mennonites migrated to the Russian Ukraine. There they established large, self-governing colonies and were not required to participate in the military.

Their favorable contract with the Russian government was threatened in the 1870s when, responding to a rising spirit of nationalism in Russia, the czar greatly modified the agreement under which the Mennonites had settled. Many of them, believing their religion and culture were in jeopardy, decided to leave. Eighteen thousand of the fifty thousand Dutch Mennonites emigrated to North America. Central Kansas became home to a large portion of the immigrants.

About the same time the Dutch Mennonites moved from Prussia to Russia, a small group of Swiss Mennonites left France and the German Palatinate to settle in Eastern Europe. They found a home near the Polish border in the Russian province of Volhynia. (See my book, *The Heritage of the Swiss Volhynian Mennonites*, Conrad Press, Waterloo, Ontario, 1981.)

The Swiss colonists who, by 1874, numbered between eight and nine hundred people, participated en masse in the great migration of Mennonites from Russia to North America. About one half of the Swiss group settled in central Kansas where they were surrounded by their coreligionists of Dutch origin.

In the interest of historical authenticity I have given Swiss-Volhynian names to the fictional characters in the novel. Since the members of the community share only a few family names, it is necessary to assure readers that all characters and situations are fictional and are in no sense meant to be biographical. Several situations, however, are based on historical incidents which are here altered and fictionalized. While the characters are purely fictional, many represent a composite of people I have known.

Solomon Stucky
Brighton, Ontario
1983

10

Part One

JONAS
1917-1918

1

The sun was not yet high enough to dry the dew on the wheat stubble and the dewdrops sparkled like diamonds as Jonas, riding on the gangplow, drove the four-horse team into the field. The heavy harnesses of thick leather and steel buckles squeaked in rhythm, and the chains, hanging from the ends of the traces where they were attached to the singletrees, jangled musically as the great Percherons walked side by side through the stubble field.

Above the sound of the marching team Jonas could hear the piercing melody of numerous meadowlarks as they competed with one another to determine which one could most loudly proclaim the beauty of the morning. The sun, a brilliant orange globe just above the eastern horizon, illuminated everything with a golden glow, turning the flat Kansas prairie landscape into a fairyland of ethereal, breathtaking beauty. The smell of dew-wet wheat stubble, the sweet fragrance of wild roses blooming in the fencerow, the pungent odor of the horses and their well-oiled harnesses, combined with the many other sights and sounds around him, gave Jonas a feeling of joyful well-being.

The well-fed horses, rested and refreshed after a Sunday in the pasture, walked along briskly with their heads high. The two geldings, Dick and Duke, were in the middle, and the two mares, Sasha and Dolly, were on the ends. The mares had foaled that spring, and the two colts, now four months old, were running in circles ahead of the team, kicking up their heels and playing.

Jonas and his team moved along beside the barbed wire fence at the south end of the field until they came to a post with a white cloth tied to its top. Jonas spoke to the horses and pulled on the right rein, bringing them to a ninety-degree turn, heading them due north. A half mile away, at the other end of the field, another white cloth hung from a limb of a tree in the osage orange hedge which formed the northern boundary of the field. The two cloths were the same distance from the western boundary of the rectangular eighty-acre field, and were placed there as a guide so the plowman could make a straight furrow across the long field.

The white cloths had been put in place the day before by Jonas's father, Big Jake Schrag or *Grosse Jakob* as the older people called him. Mennonites did only essential farm work on Sundays, such as feeding the animals and milking the cows, but sometimes Big Jake bent the rules a little. He usually took a leisurely stroll around his fields on Sunday afternoons while he planned the work for the coming week. Surely there was no harm in counting your steps as you walked, and, if you just happened to have a couple of white rags in your pocket, it surely wasn't work to tie them onto a branch of a hedge tree and the top of a fence post.

Making sure the horses were faced directly toward the white marker on the far end of the field, Jonas spoke to them and gave the reins a shake to signal them to start. At the same time he pushed the foot-operated lever that dropped the two shiny plowshares into the ground as the horses moved forward. As they moved across the field, he, from time to time, glanced down to see with satisfaction that the plow was set at the right depth and was working well. It was always a pleasure for him to see the rich black earth rise up over the moldboards and turn over, burying the stubble. He could take only a quick sideways glance now and then on this first trip through the field because he had to keep his eye on the white marker ahead so that the first furrow would be perfectly straight.

When he came to the osage orange hedge at the end of the field, Jonas pushed the foot lever again to lift the plowshares out of the ground and brought the horses around to a full one-hundred-eighty degree turn. He got off the plow and went around to the horses' heads and, stroking each on the face, spoke to them, all the while checking quickly over their harnesses and collars to make sure everything was in place and the horses were working comfortably. Satisfied that all was well, he looked back and saw that the long ribbon of plowed land was a straight black line through the yellow stubble.

Jonas remounted the plow and started the return trip across the field. He still could not let his attention wander too much because the return trip on that first round also demanded skill to keep the plow going straight as the soil was turned to mound up over the soil turned over on the first trip across the field. Once the first round was completed, the plowing was easier because, as the soil was turned, it fell into the furrow made on the previous round. Each time Jonas came to the end and turned the horses around for the return trip, he stopped them for a minute or two to rest. He had learned that the time was more than made up in the faster pace of the horses as they looked forward to a rest at each end of the field.

Grossvatter° Schrag, a gentle man who loved horses, had taught Jonas a great deal about how to work with them. Jonas, too, loved horses and was grateful to his grandfather for teaching him how to work with and care for them. Big Jake had little of the patience needed for working with horses. While working with them he urged them on in a rough voice and permitted them to rest only when he saw they were becoming winded. When Jonas, under his grandfather's tutoring, had begun to plow, Big Jake, always impatient to get the work done, objected to letting the horses rest every time they came to the end of the field. However, when Grossvatter pointed out one day

---

°Grandfather

15

that Jonas had more land plowed at the end of the day than Big Jake had, who was plowing with the other four-horse team, and that Jonas's team was not as tired, he let the matter drop.

All morning Jonas and his big draft animals moved back and forth across the field. At first the frisky colts ran with them, but after a few rounds they were tired and lay down to rest in the shade of the hedge on the north end of the field. They lay there while their mothers made one trip to the far end, but on the return trip, as they saw the mares approaching, the colts jumped up and ran to them to nurse. Jonas didn't allow the team to stop, however, and the frustrated colts ran alongside, snorting, nuzzling at the mares' flanks, and whinnying, until the team reached the end and made the turn for the return trip. This time the team got a longer rest as the mares nursed their colts.

As Jonas plowed, he could see his brother Chris plowing with the other team in the quarter section across the road. He was working on the far side of the quarter and was plowing east and west. Grossvatter Schrag had tried to teach Chris how to work with horses too, but, impatient like his father, and not loving horses the way Jonas did, he would never be a good horseman. At the end of each day, though, he usually had almost as much land plowed as Jonas. This was not true at first, but one day Jonas overheard Big Jake tell Chris not to yell at the horses so much and to let them rest at each end of the field.

Just when his stomach began to tell him it must be noon, Jonas's little sister, Annie, appeared at the corner of the field near the house waving a big, white dish towel. This was the signal that it was dinner time. On reaching the end of the field Jonas turned the grateful horses toward the barn. He saw that Chris, too, had seen the signal and was bringing his team in.

Both teams reached the big yard between the house and barn at the same time. All eight horses stood in a row as they were unhitched. The two young men worked quickly and efficiently unhooking traces, removing jockey-poles and restraining straps, and dropping the plow tongues and neck-yokes to

16

the ground. As each animal was freed from the rest, its bridle was removed and hung on the hame projecting above his collar. One by one the freed horses walked over to the big, round water tank, drank thirstily, and then went quietly into the barn to stand, each in its own stall, to wait for the noon feeding. After all were unhitched, Jonas and Chris went into the feed alley in front of the long row of horses, and dipping metal pails into the oat bin, gave each horse a full ration of oats. They put a generous forkful of timothy hay into each manger and secured each horse in its stall by slipping a halter over its head.

On the way to the house Chris said, "Wonder what's for dinner. I'm so hungry I feel like my belly button's glued to my backbone."

Jonas laughed and wondered what had happened to the thick slices of ham, the mound of fried potatoes, the four eggs, and four thick slices of bread with butter and jam Chris had eaten for breakfast. The younger of the two, Chris was almost a head taller than Jonas and outweighed him by fifty pounds. It seemed he was always hungry. With a physical build like his father, he was already referred to by some as Big Chris.

They went through the screen door into the closed-in back porch where they saw that someone had placed a full bucket of water on the wash table. They dipped water from it, filling the two big pans on the table, and washed the black dust from their hands and faces. After taking turns at the roller towel on the wall beside the table, they picked up the pans and, opening the screen door, tossed the muddied water out into the backyard.

The smell of food coming from the kitchen made Jonas realize that he was probably as hungry as Chris had said he was. Entering the kitchen, they could see that dinner was ready. In the middle of the table was a big platter filled with chunks of boiled beef that had been canned when they butchered the steer last spring. Another platter was piled high with thick slices of fresh bread, and there was a big bowl of creamed peas. The white enameled pitcher was filled with cool milk. There was also a plate of butter and a jar of wild plum jam. As they came in, their mother was at the stove testing the boiling potatoes to see if they were soft. Satisfied, she drained the water from the large kettle and brought it, steaming, to the table.

Big Jake was already seated at the head of the table and the three little girls, Annie, Lydia, and Emma, were standing at their places next to the wall. When Elizabeth Schrag placed the big kettle of potatoes on the table, she motioned to her sons to take their chairs as she took her place at the foot of the table opposite Big Jake.

As soon as everyone was seated, with all heads bowed and hands folded, Big Jake repeated the ritual prayer, "*Kom Herr Jesu sei unser Gast und segne was Du uns beschert hast. Amen.*"°

These were the only words spoken during the meal while everyone concentrated on the business of eating. For years Big Jake had discouraged conversation at the table. The children had long ago learned that any idle chatter would result in a look of glaring disapproval from their giant of a father.

The difference in age between the boys, who were nineteen and twenty-one, and the girls who were eight, six, and four, was the result of a diphtheria tragedy that struck the family a few months before Annie, the oldest of the three little girls, was born. The family had consisted of six children, and within a period of two weeks that winter, the youngest four had died.

Elizabeth had not been able to cope with the horror of it. While her own family and Big Jake's family had tried to help her overcome her grief, she withdrew more and more into herself, and, avoiding others, spent her time in unending work. Small and thin, she had become even thinner, as, hollow-eyed, she went about her incessant work, her prominent cheek bones accentuating her sunken cheeks. Big Jake, grieving as any father would, had finally put away his grief and had not been able to understand Elizabeth's continued despondence. Out of

---

° *Come, Lord Jesus, be our guest, and bless what you have bestowed on us.*

18

frustration, he gradually withdrew so that now they spoke and shared little.

Over the years, as the girls demanded more of Elizabeth's attention and more time had separated her from the tragedy, some of the hurt had gone out of her eyes, but a way of life had been established.

As soon as Jonas and Chris had finished eating, they left the table. Retrieving their straw hats from the hooks on the wall of the back porch, they went out to carry water to the hogs. The hot Kansas summers made pigs uncomfortable and they needed lots of water to give them relief from the heat. Noticing that the big stock tank was less than half full, Jonas released the lever that started the windmill pumping water. The winds had been calm in the early morning, but by midmorning the south wind was blowing hard as it did almost every day through the summer.

When the hogs had enough water, the young men went to the barn, and, slipping the bridles on the horses' heads, brought them out, each leading two of the big animals. They led them to the tank for another drink and then to one of the plows where they were rehitched in preparation for the afternoon work. After hitching up one team, they got the other four horses out and hitched them to the other plow. While Chris started his team back to the south quarter, Jonas went to the house to ask his mother to keep an eye on the stock tank which would be full in a couple of hours, and to tell Annie to shut off the windmill. Stepping through the kitchen door, he saw Elizabeth washing dishes in the dishpan on her worktable. Big Jake was still sitting at the dining table smoking his smelly pipe filled with his homegrown tobacco. He was reading the *Mennonitische Blätter* spread out before him on the blue and white checkered oilcloth. He didn't look up.

About an hour after Jonas went back to the field, he was making the turn at the north end when he saw Big Jake driving to town in his buggy. His little mare, in spite of the heat, was going at a full gallop. Big Jake had bought the mare years

19

before from some horse dealers who made a business of capturing wild horses in the West, partially breaking them, then herding them farther east and selling them to prairie farmers. For some reason Big Jake seemed to enjoy the challenge involved in harnessing and hitching up the half-wild mare. He usually covered the first two miles of the trip to town at a full gallop, and the last two at a fast trot. He had named the mare *Malagetz*, which was a Russian word describing a "go-getter."

When he got to Prairie Ridge he would tie his mare to the hitching rail in the shade of the cottonwood trees beside the ice plant. Several summers ago he had discovered that the owner of the ice plant kept a stock of beer in a corner of the insulated ice storage room. Next to it was a little room with tables where men could sit and visit and drink ice-cold beer. Now that he had two grown sons to work in the fields, he rather enjoyed his position of "owner-manager" of the farm. Almost every day during the summer months he found some reason to go to town. One day he would take a spare set of plowshares to Bill Thiele's blacksmith shop for sharpening, and the next day he would have to go in to pick them up. Another day he needed a buckle or two from Harness Schrag's harness shop. Hardly a day passed when there was not a good reason to go to town.

The almost daily visits with his friends in town did not mean that the farm was not efficiently managed. Big Jake was constantly aware of what needed to be done, and had done a good job of training his sons in all aspects of farm work so that, now they were grown, he could take life a little easier.

Watching his father disappear down the road in a cloud of dust, Jonas returned to his thoughts. He spent a lot of his time thinking about the war. It had been going on in Europe for three years, and now America was in it too. Some of the young men in the church had already been drafted and were in Camp Funston at Fort Riley wearing soldiers' uniforms. Because they were Mennonites, they didn't have to carry guns or be taught how to kill, but they still had to join the army and wear uniforms.

Jonas remembered all the stories his grandfather Schrag told him about life in Russia, how they hated to leave their village in Volhynia back in 1874, but they knew they had to leave when the czar said their young men would have to join the army. All of the Swiss Mennonites in Volhynia left their homes that year and came to America. A lot of the other Mennonites in Volhynia and in south Russia left too, but when the czar realized all the Mennonites were going to leave, he said their young men could join the *Forsteidienst°* instead of the army, so more than half of them stayed. Now, here in America, the young men had to join the army and wear the uniforms of soldiers.

Jonas knew that any day now he would get a letter from the government telling him he was being drafted. Within the past two weeks several of his cousins had received such letters and were given two weeks to report for a physical examination. The only way one could get an exemption to stay on the farm was if he was the only son old enough to work. Chris was nineteen, so Jonas knew they wouldn't let him stay on the farm.

For the past year he and Anna Gering had been going together on Sunday evenings to the *Jugendverein°°* and evening preaching. Since the beginning of summer they had spent almost every Sunday afternoon together. Buffalo Creek ran through the Gering farm, and Jonas and Anna would sometimes walk together along its banks, or sit under a cottonwood tree beside the creek and talk. Lately the talk had been mostly of the war and what they would do if Jonas was drafted. They talked of marriage, but could not make plans because of the war, and also Jonas didn't know how Big Jake would react to his wanting to get married. Even though he was twenty-one and considered by law to be a man in his own right, the only way he knew how to support a wife and family was by farming. His father owned the land, the machinery, and the horses, so

---

° Forestry service.
°°Youth meeting.

he had the final say about when Jonas could get married.

Big Jake had spent about an hour in the ice plant visiting with several of his friends who also had discovered the pleasures of leisure time because they had grown sons to do their plowing. Now, as Big Jake approached the buggy, ready to go home, Malagetz impatiently pawed the ground, anxious to be on her way. Standing well back in case she should decide to kick at him, Big Jake untied the reins from the footrest on the floor of the buggy and, holding them tightly, approached her head to untie the hitching strap that tied her to the rail. He kept an eye on her long, yellow teeth which she bared, glaring at him as if daring him to make a false move. He untied the hitching strap, all the while holding tightly to the reins in case she decided to bolt. With one hand he fastened the strap to a ring on the right hame. Man and mare continued to glare at one another while Big Jake slowly backed up toward the buggy. When he reached the right spot, he leaped into the buggy seat. At the same instant the mare made a great backward leap, driving the buggy backward several yards. This being a regular ritual, Big Jake braced himself for the forward leap and sharp turn, which started them on their way home.

Just after passing the sign that read, "Prairie Ridge, City Limits," he heard a Ford coming up behind him. He braced himself but let Malagetz have her head. Spurred by terror, she ran, ears laid back, eyes rolling in their sockets, frothing at the mouth. Big Jake grinned behind his salt-and-pepper beard and wondered how far they would get this time before the Ford caught up with them. Without turning to look, he knew it was his cousin Pete driving the Ford. Pete had been at the ice plant with him and was getting ready to leave at the time Big Jake left. A mile and a half out of town, a full quarter-mile farther than the last time, the Ford pulled alongside. Big Jake fought to keep the mare on the road and when the rear end of the Ford was even with Malagetz's head, Pete pushed the retard spark lever down and quickly up again, causing the Ford to backfire. The terrified mare stopped so quickly her hooves slid

22

along the dirt road and she sat down. Up almost immediately, standing on her hind legs and pawing the air, she attempted to turn around. By sheer strength Big Jake kept her from turning. She dropped on all four feet, heaving and staring after the speeding Ford.

"Just wait! I'll get even with you, you *verstunkene Hans Wurst!*"° Big Jake called after his retreating cousin, but he grinned as he said it.

The little mare was trembling, and Big Jake held her still for a few minutes before signaling her to start again. She walked for a while but soon began to trot of her own accord.

"As soon as this war is over, and you can buy them again, I'm going to have one of those Fords, and then I won't have to put up with you anymore," Big Jake told the mare. Most people wondered why he kept the malicious creature, but his family knew he had genuine affection for her. She had foaled twice, each time with difficulty, and each time Big Jake had spent the entire night with her, helping her through the ordeal.

As he went toward home he took careful note of the amount of plowing each neighbor had done. Passing Helmut Krehbiel's quarter section, he saw Helmut out on his plow. The Krehbiels had ten daughters and not one son. Helmut was older than Jake, and he had to do his own plowing.

It was a good year, Big Jake thought as he rode along observing the thick wheat stubble in the large, level fields. He thought of his own granaries piled to the rafters with the golden grain. Never in history had the price of wheat been so high. When the fall planting was done and before they began to pick corn, he and the boys would haul the wheat to the elevator and sell it.

Just before he came to his own land he passed the quarter section belonging to old Jim Atkins. The land was, of course, as good as all the land in the area, but didn't produce as well because, as everyone knew, these *Englishers* or Yankees just

---

°Smelly sausage.

couldn't farm as well as the Mennonites. The farm looked poor now because the buildings needed repair and weeds were growing all over the yard. The old man just couldn't keep up anymore. Big Jake was sure he would be ready to sell after next year's harvest. Jonas was running after Gering Hanzul's Anna, and it probably wouldn't be long before he would want to get married and he would need a farm to get started on. If he bought the Atkins' land adjoining his own, he'd have one large farm with two sets of buildings. For a few years Jonas could continue to work on both farms to pay Big Jake back for helping him get started. He would turn the whole thing over to the two boys then and buy a house in town. With the landlord's share of three quarter sections of crops, he would have more than enough for himself without having to work at all. He could, of course, drive out to the farm in his Ford any time he felt like it to see that the boys were doing things the way they should be done.

Coming now to where his own land lay on both sides of the road, he saw that Jonas's strip of plowed land was so wide that another round or two would bring it to the west edge, and he would have to start another strip. When he reached the driveway by the house he turned into the field and drove along the fence until he reached the post with the white cloth tied to it. Without getting out of the buggy, he untied the white cloth, turned, and drove back to the edge of the plowed portion of the field. He got out of the buggy and tied Malagetz to a post. Pacing off several hundred yards, he retied the cloth to another post, walked back and untied the mare, who was now too tired to play her game with him. Driving to the north end of the field he changed the marker to correspond with the one on the south end. When the second strip of plowed land was as wide as the first, there would still be a wide strip of unplowed stubble between them, and Jonas would then make his rounds counter-clockwise until the plowed sections met. Big Jake drove back to the yard, out the driveway and across the road, where he changed the markers for Chris.

24

Back in the yard, he backed his buggy into the shed, un-hitched Malagetz, and took her to the barn. He tied her in her stall, removed her light harness, and hung it on its peg on the wall. Looking along the long row of stalls, he decided that the next time it rained and the boys couldn't plow, they could clean the barn.

2

The next Sunday morning Jonas and Chris hitched up the team of chestnut geldings to the surrey for Big Jake, Elizabeth, and the three little girls to ride to church. The horses had been born on the farm of a mare that was half bronco and half Morgan. The sire was a Belgian, so the team was big enough to be used for field work and at the same time fast enough for the family surrey. When the horses were ready to go Chris tied them to the hitching post in front of the house, and went up to his room to dress for church. Jonas went back into the barn to bring out his own horse. The four-year-old sorrel with a white blaze and long, flowing mane and tail was Jonas's pride and joy. The horse's mother was Big Jake's Malagetz, and the sire was a Standardbred horse that had won many races in the East before Big Jake's cousin Pete bought him for stud service. When the colt was a day old, Big Jake told Jonas the baby animal was his. Jonas named him Blaze.

When the colt was old enough, Jonas spent all his spare time training him. He sent off for a book on horse training, and by the time Blaze was three years old, he was a five-gaited horse. At given signals he would walk, trot, canter, pace, or gallop. The fall he was two-and-one-half, Jonas found an old buggy which he bought for a few dollars. He kept it in the barn, and through the winter modified and restored it to mint condition, so that by spring he had a "courting buggy" that was the envy of most of the young men in the community. The shiny black buggy and the proud, high-stepping, arch-necked horse brought people to their windows as Jonas and his rig passed by.

Bringing his rig up behind the surrey, he didn't bother to tie his horse, knowing he would stand perfectly still until his return. As Jonas went toward the house his parents and little sisters came out to get into the surrey. "Don't be late," his mother said as she came down the steps.

It didn't take Jonas long to wash the horse smell off his hands and run upstairs to change into his Sunday clothes. He had shaved before breakfast. When he nicked his chin with the straightedge razor, he almost wished the church still required men to wear beards the way they used to. All the older men still wore them because they wanted to, not because the church *ordnung*° required it.

Chris yelled from downstairs for him to hurry. Jonas quickly tied his bow tie, looked himself over in the mirror, and patted some after-shave on his face. He put on his derby hat as he ran downstairs. Chris was already outside and going toward the buggy.

The two young men were dressed almost alike with light-colored striped shirts with white collars, brown suspenders, narrow-legged brown pants, black shoes, brown bow ties, and brown derby hats. The weather was too warm for jackets. The grandfathers and grandmothers complained that the young people dressed too worldly, and that the young men looked like dandies. When they were young, the church *ordnung* required that everyone dress alike in homemade clothes with hooks and eyes, and not try to make themselves look like the fashionable people of the world.

The high-stepping Blaze caught up to the family surrey on the main street of Prairie Ridge and followed it to the church on the south end of town. The yard on both sides of the church was filled with buggies, surreys, a number of Fords, and several bigger automobiles. After tying the horses to the hitching rail

---

° Rules.

along the row of cottonwood trees north of the church, the family started to walk toward the front of the building. They could sense that something was wrong. Ordinarily on Sunday morning in summer, before Sunday school started, people would cluster in small groups talking and laughing together. Today the entire congregation crowded in front of the church. Talking was serious, low-pitched, and intense. Suddenly Preacher John Kaufman appeared standing in the doorway, announcing that it was time to come in. The congregation filed in silently and quickly, mothers shushing little children. Preacher John stood at the front holding before him with both hands a big piece of rolled-up yellow cardboard. When everyone was seated and silent, he looked at the sea of expectant faces before him and unrolled the big cardboard scroll. "By now most of you are aware that when I came to church early this morning, I found this sign nailed to the door of the church. Many of you cannot read the English words, so I will translate them for you." As he translated the crude, red-crayon lettering on the two-by-three-foot, yellow cardboard, he held it up so all could see.

From now on
only English
will be spoken
in this church.
German is the
language of the Hun.
This is America!

After everyone who could read the English words had had a chance to see it, Preacher John laid the sign, back side up, on the platform behind him. Turning again to face the silent congregation he said, "Forty-three years ago we came to America. Grateful we were then, and grateful we are now that this country opened its doors to us and allowed us to live in peace. We have lived here in peace these many years and have been allowed to teach our children God's Word in the language of our fathers. We do not object to our children learning English in the schools, and we know that someday, perhaps, English will be the language spoken here in our church. But that time is not yet.

"People who do not know the history of our people think that because we speak the German language we support the German state. They do not understand that for almost four hundred years we have said we live only by the rules of Christ's kingdom and are not interested in the kingdoms of this world. Our Lord Jesus has told us to render unto Caesar the things that are Caesar's and to God the things that are God's. Thus we gladly pay our taxes, but when the law of the land is contrary to the law of God, we must obey God rather than men. When the law of the land says we must kill our brothers who are also created in the image of God, it is contrary to the law of God.

"In time of war, people are taught they must hate the people of the country on whom war is being waged. We happen to speak the same language the people of Germany speak, so we too have become the objects of that hatred, especially since we refuse to take up weapons against the people of Germany.

"In the forty-three years that the German-speaking Mennonites from Russia have lived in the prairie states of America, we have earned the respect of our fellow Americans. Newspaper articles have praised our industry and thrift, and, indeed, men in government, in the very halls of Congress, have spoken of us as ideal citizens. Now, suddenly, in this year of 1917, we have become a threat to our neighbors and are being called a people unfit to live in America.

"We have lived in peace and prosperity for so long that we have forgotten what our ancestors, the Anabaptists of Switzerland, never had a chance to forget: that to be a true follower of Christ is to suffer the ridicule and scorn of the world and even to be ready at all times for the martyrs' crown.

"All of you born before 1874 were a part of the great migration out of Russia. That migration and the reasons for it are a part of our spiritual heritage. As a people we said then we must obey God rather than man, and we gave up everything we had to go to an unknown land almost halfway around the world where we believed we could, in complete freedom, follow the commands of Christ. We were right to do as we did.

"Now we are faced with the same problem, and we have, as a people, decided to stay where we are and weather the storm, rather than emigrate again. God grant the decision will prove to be the right one. I pray that our decision was not made on the basis of our vast land holdings and the price of wheat." This brought a restless shuffling of feet, and those with the largest farms seemed to stare hardest at the floor. Some thought, but of course would never voice their thoughts, that Preacher John, with his single, indifferently farmed quarter section, could talk about emigration. But then they thought of all the work he did for the church, for which he received nothing, and they felt guilty.

"Be that as it may," Preacher John continued, "the decision to remain has been made. We can only pray that the war and the killing will be over soon and with it the hate people feel for each other. We must remember, no matter how much we are provoked, that we are followers of our Lord Jesus Christ who said, 'Love your enemies, do good to those who hate you, bless those who curse you, pray for those who abuse you.' As we come in daily contact with those who hate us for our German language and our refusal to participate in war, we must remember that love is stronger than hate, and that only by loving our neighbor can he be won for Christ."

Glancing at the clock on the wall, he said, "I'm afraid I've taken up the time usually spent on the opening exercises for Sunday school, so we will start our classes, but first let us turn to our *Gesang Buch mit Noten*° and sing *Ein feste Burg ist unser Gott*."°° After a few notes from the pump organ the congregation found the page and began singing Luther's powerful

---

°Songbook with notes.
°°A Mighty Fortress Is Our God.

hymn. The German words had a special impact on them today. With great feeling the large congregation, in four-part harmony, sang:

> Ein feste Burg ist unser Gott, ein gute Wehr und Waffen.
> Er hilft uns frei aus aller Not, die uns jetzt hat betroffen.
> Der alt böse Feind mit Ernst er's jetzt meint;
> gross Macht und viel List sein grausam Rüstung ist;
> auf Erd ist nicht seins gleichen.°

After singing all four verses, the congregation stood for prayer, and then dispersed for Sunday school classes.

When the church service ended over two hours later, there was the usual visiting among families in the churchyard, but conversations were subdued.

Grossvatter and Grossmutter Schrag came to Sunday dinner at Big Jake's house. They followed the surrey in their old buggy. They still used many Russian words, and they called their buggy a drozhki. Jonas and Chris drove on ahead and had Blaze in the barn before the others arrived. After the surrey and drozhki pulled into the yard, the young men took care of the horses while the others went into the house.

Finished with the horses, they crossed the yard to the house where they washed their hands at the table on the closed-in back porch. They breathed deeply with mouth-watering anticipation the aroma of roast chicken coming through the kitchen window. Grossmutter and Elizabeth worked in the kitchen while Annie set the table with the help of her little sisters. Jonas and Chris went through the dining room to the parlor where Big Jake and Grossvatter were sitting and talking.

Jonas was always amazed at the different ways Big Jake acted and talked under different circumstances. He was one kind of person around his wife and children, another around his friends in town, and yet another in the presence of his father and mother.

° See page 238.

He was always mild-mannered and pleasant around his parents, 'and treated them with the respect the gentle old people deserved. When his father talked of life in the old country, Big Jake listened attentively, and occasionally asked questions to encourage the old man to talk, even though he had heard the stories many times over.

Today the conversation concerned the incident at church. Not that it had come as a great surprise. Ever since America had entered the war in April they had noticed a difference in their non-Mennonite neighbors. People who usually spoke to them on the street now looked the other way. Posters in front of and in the post office showed pictures of young men in uniform and some of them made reference to "slackers" who had not yet joined up to fight the Germans. Newspaper editorials and articles said nasty things about the Germans living in America who refused to fight, but this was the first time a Mennonite church in their area had been directly addressed this way.

Jonas and Chris took chairs across the room from their grandfather and listened as he talked. Sitting in the rocking chair, he rocked slowly. "It was not like this in Russia. The people who lived in the villages around us didn't hate us because we didn't believe in war. They didn't want war either. Many of our neighbors were Lutherans who spoke German as we did. Many were Jews who had no love for the czar's government, and even the Russians around us didn't concern themselves with the government in St. Petersburg. At one time Volhynia had been a part of the Polish nation, and the people didn't seem to care if the government was in St. Petersburg or Warsaw.

"Now America is at war with Germany and the people think that to live in America we have to hate the German language and the German people. Why can't we be left alone to care for our farms and live by the rules of our *Gemeinden*° the way we

---

°Congregations.

32

did in our villages in Russia? Of course," he shrugged, "things changed in Russia too when the czar said our young men would have to be soldiers. So we came to America where they told us there would be no war, and now our young men are sent away to the army to wear soldiers' uniforms.

"One day last week I was in Prairie Ridge when the train came in and a soldier got off. He looked familiar, and when I got closer I saw it was Hannes Vetter's Andrushka." The old man's voice broke as he said the name, and Jonas, Chris, and Big Jake looked at the floor as tears streamed down the old man's wrinkled cheeks into his white beard.

Elizabeth appeared at the door and announced that dinner was ready.

Sunday dinners when Grossvatter and Grossmutter were there were much different than when the family ate alone. Before the meal started, Grossvatter led the family in prayer. It was not the ritual prayer tersely repeated by Big Jake at each meal. The old man talked to God intimately about the things that were troubling him and thanked him for what he had given them.

After the prayer Grossmutter took over. She was a big-boned, heavy woman who seemed to be always smiling. She talked to each of the little girls across the table, and drew from each a shy response. They were so used to eating in silence that they found it difficult to speak at the table, even though they could see their father smiling through his chewing. "And you, Christi," she said, "When are you going to stop growing? You are already taller than your papa and soon you'll be looking down on him." Chris grinned, happy for the attention, but didn't answer. Next she turned to Jonas who was sitting beside her. "Jonas, each Sunday at evening preaching I see you come in with Gering Hanzul's Anna, and I think 'what a nice couple.' When are you two going to be announced and be married? I want some great-grandchildren."

Chris sniggered across the table, and nudged Jonas on the shin with his boot. Everyone in the room was smiling broadly.

Even Big Jake was grinning into his plate. Jonas lowered his head and continued eating, aware that his face had turned beet-red. Realizing she had embarrassed him, Grossmutter changed the subject, but not her happy mood, and soon had everyone responding to her questions.

After dinner when Jonas put on his hat preparing to go out, Grossmutter, knowing he was going to see Anna, patted him on the shoulder and said, "Anna is a good girl, she will be a fine woman for you." Jonas nodded, smiling at her and went out the door.

It was a warm sun-filled Sunday afternoon. The wind, instead of the pushing, tearing force it was most summer afternoons, was a gentle caressing breeze. Jonas and Anna had, for a long time, been sitting under their favorite cottonwood tree beside the creek. They had stopped talking and were watching the small herd of red and white shorthorns lying in the shade across the creek idly chewing their cud. Jonas picked up a small twig of dead cottonwood in his hands, and, breaking off small pieces, began tossing them into the deep pool beneath the bank, watching the silvery ripples form rings that grew ever larger until they disappeared in the smooth surface of the murky water. The silence was complete except for the rustle of the leaves above them and the faint buzzing of insects. When the last of the twig fragments had been tossed into the water, Jonas turned to Anna and said, "Let's talk to Preacher John tonight."

Anna reached out and put her hand on Jonas's arm. "Ach Jonas, you know that's what I want more than anything else, but we still don't know what will happen with the draft. And what about your papa?"

As she was talking Jonas stood up, and, reaching down, grasped her hands and pulled her to her feet. He put two fingers over her lips to signal no more talking. Holding her close, he said, "I love you, Anna."

She responded simply, "I love you, Jonas." Though some of the conversation that afternoon had been in English, this last exchange was in German. All their lives sacred truths had been transmitted in German.

Continuing in German, Jonas said, "If I leave now to go home to help Chris with the chores, I'll get there before Grossmutter and Grossvatter are gone. I'll go directly to the parlor where they're visiting, and I'll tell papa right out that we're going to talk to Preacher John tonight, and we'll be announced next Sunday. Papa's always in a good mood when his parents are there, and if he starts to give me trouble, Grossmutter will bring him around."

At the close of the service the next Sunday, Preacher John made the announcement. "Two weeks from this day "Jonas Schrag and Anna Gering will stand before the congregation and, in the presence of God and the *Gemeinde*, repeat the holy vows of matrimony." Jonas could hear the murmur of approval through the congregation as he stared straight ahead, feeling that everyone was looking at him.

After the service, as soon as he and Anna could get away from all the congratulators, they got into Jonas's rig and drove to Anna's house where Jonas endured the good-natured ribbing of Anna's young brothers while Anna helped her mother and sisters prepare dinner. After the dinner, at which everyone in the large family seemed to be talking at once, Jonas and Anna got back into the buggy and spent the afternoon going from house to house, visiting relatives.

According to custom, the ritual, including the announcement in church, the Sunday dinner, and the afternoon visiting, was repeated the following Sunday. The second Sunday they visited those relatives missed on the first.

On the third Sunday in September, at the end of the morning service, they were married. After the benediction, Preacher John led them outside the church ahead of the congregation where they stood to receive the congratulations and well-wishes of the people as they filed past them. When everyone had had a chance to shake their hands, the young couple went to their rig and led the procession to the Gering farm. No invitations were sent out, but none were needed. It was taken for granted that following a wedding, the bride's parents would host the wedding dinner for the entire congregation.

Close relatives had spent several days helping the family prepare for the feast. Dozens of long tables, consisting of sawhorses and planks, had been set up in the shade of the elm and cottonwood trees between the house and the road. Ten days before the big day, a steer had been killed, quartered, and hung in a special room in the ice plant in town to cool and age. The day before the wedding it was cut up into large roasts and distributed among relatives for roasting. Each family brought baskets filled with food and eating utensils.

While the women worked, getting the food ready, the Sunday school song leader led the congregation in several songs that everyone could sing without songbooks. They sang *Gott ist die Liebe*° and *Nun danket alle Gott.*°° After a men's quartet sang several numbers, the food was ready and Preacher John asked God's blessing on the food and festivities.

Small children sat on benches around a low, improvised table under an elm tree. Mothers and older sisters began filling their plates. Adults lined the food-laden tables and began filling their plates with thick slices of roast beef, cold home-cured ham, piles of boiled potatoes, and cooked vegetables. Stacks of homemade bread waited to be spread with an abundant variety of jams and jellies. Large dishpans, piled high with poppy seed rolls, and all kinds of cakes and pies covered another table. Several twenty-gallon stone crocks filled with lemonade stood beside waiting glasses.

A number of people had brought rocking chairs for the old people, who now formed two circles, one for the grossmutters and another for the grossvatters, where they happily visited together. Their conversations were mostly concerning incidents of their youth in their village of Kotosufka far away.

° God Is Love.
°° Now Thank We All Our God.

The large crowd divided itself into groups whose common interests brought them together for conversation. Recently married couples sat together in a group while they ate, but as soon as they were finished, the young married men drifted off to watch and then participate in one of several games of horseshoe that had been started.

Big Jake was part of a group of middle-aged men who, after discussing the relative merits of the various brands of farm machinery in use on their farms, brought the conversation around to the incident of the sign nailed to the church door. Several were of the opinion that if the Mennonites stuck together and had nothing to do with anyone else, everything would be all right. Most of the stores in Prairie Ridge were owned by Mennonites, so no Mennonite business should go to outsiders. Someone else pointed out that the only businessmen in the town that weren't Mennonites were the two Syrian brothers with their little clothing and drygoods store, and the old Yankee who sold and fixed clocks. The blacksmith was a Lutheran, and he spoke German just as the Mennonites did. None of these men nailed the sign to the church door, and, anyway, how about the business of turning the other cheek?

The conversation drifted to other things, and Big Jake was just as glad because he didn't want to be questioned about his occasional trips to the town of Brinton where there were no Mennonite merchants, but where the local storekeepers often sold necessary items for less than the Mennonites charged him in Prairie Ridge.

About five o'clock the women and older girls began gathering up the dishes each family had brought, putting them in baskets for the men to carry to the surreys or cars. It was time to go home for the evening chores which had to be done before getting ready for evening preaching.

This being his wedding day, Jonas was excused from evening chores, so he stayed at the Gering home until it was time to go to church again.

Unlike the old days, when men and boys sat on one side of

the church and the women and girls on the other side, married couples now sat together. Jonas and Anna chose a bench where other young married couples were sitting. By sitting close together and keeping their hands on the bench between them, no one could see they were holding hands.

As soon as they could get away after the service, they started for home in Jonas's rig. Blaze, anxious to be in his own stall after being gone all day, would have galloped at full speed, but Jonas concentrated on holding him down to a steady trot. Anna sat with her hands clasped tightly together in her lap. The occasional verbal exchanges were designed to hide the turmoil each felt, anticipating their wedding night.

The room that would be theirs was the big square one in the southwest corner of the second floor of the large farmhouse. Until now the room was never needed, so it had never been furnished. One day during the past week, Anna, her parents, and her oldest brother had gone to town to the store with the big sign over the door that said, "Mueller Furniture and Undertaking." Anna's father and her brother Pete went in the wagon while Anna and her mother drove a buggy. They tied the horse with the buggy to the hitching rail in front, but the wagon was taken to the back of the store. Inside, the two women picked out bedroom furniture. They chose an ornate brass bed with coil springs and mattress, a large dresser with a bevel-edged mirror, a small marble topped oak table, and a big porcelain water pitcher and matching basin. At Gering Hanzul's suggestion, they also bought a large comfortable looking rocking chair, and a beautiful 12-by-15 foot carpet with a floral design.

With Anna's big cedar chest already in the wagon, the men had difficulty finding room for all the new things. When they arrived at the Schrag farm, Big Jake was in town, and Jonas and Chris were out going over the fields one last time with harrows before wheat planting began.

The Gering wagon was backed up to the front porch of the house, and Elizabeth opened the seldom used front door. After speaking a few words of welcome, she went back to work in the kitchen. The three little girls stared in wide-eyed wonder as the furniture was unloaded and carried upstairs where it was arranged to Anna's satisfaction. Anna and her mother hung lace curtains at the windows, and, after making up the bed, covered it with a beautiful, hand-pieced quilt Anna's grossmutter had made for her.

Jonas was working at the far side of the south quarter and hadn't seen the Gering wagon, so he was puzzled when he came into the house after evening chores and his sisters insisted they wanted to show him something upstairs. After Annie opened the door to the big bedroom, Jonas stared in wonder. He had never seen so fine a bedroom. It stood in sharp contrast to his own sparsely furnished little room with the plain wooden bed with a *strohsack*° mattress covering the slats. Big Jake didn't believe in spending money foolishly on furniture—especially if no one but the family ever saw it.

Now, home at last on their wedding night, Anna waited on the side porch for Jonas to put his horse in the barn. She was hoping he would hurry so they could be in their own room before the family came home from church. She needn't have worried, because Jonas was thinking the same thing, and Elizabeth, who normally spoke only briefly to friends and relatives after church before going to the surrey where she waited for Big Jake, now prolonged her after-church visiting to make sure the young people would be in the privacy of their own room before she and Big Jake and the girls got home. Chris had his own rig now and wouldn't be home until later.

The next morning, after Jonas and Chris had finished the barn chores and harnessed eight horses, they washed up on the back porch. They could hear their mother and Anna talking in the kitchen as they prepared breakfast. Elizabeth was telling Anna where to find things in the cupboards, and Anna was

---

°Strawsack

talking to Elizabeth and the little girls as though conversation was an end in itself instead of something to be employed only when absolutely necessary.

When all were seated at the table and Big Jake had said his ritual prayer, Anna immediately began asking Annie and Lydia about school. They shyly answered her questions, keeping an eye on their father, not knowing whether or not they were allowed to talk. Big Jake seemed preoccupied with his food, so they began to think that, even though Anna was going to be here always, it was like having company all the time, and conversation would be allowed. However, when Annie began to volunteer something about school without being asked, her father gave her a sharp glance, and she stopped in mid-sentence. Apparently it was all right to speak when spoken to, but not to speak on your own.

Jonas, who had been amazed at Anna's talkative family, had told her about the silent meals at his own home and the general lack of conversation. Anna knew that she couldn't live that way and was determined to do what she could to change things.

Anna was only a small child when the diphtheria tragedy had struck the Schrag family, but her mother had told her that Elizabeth had been a happy, friendly person before that, but had grieved too long for her children, so that her sadness had spread like a disease through her house. Anna was determined not to let the disease overcome her but to do what she could to push it out of the house.

As soon as breakfast was over, Jonas and Chris went to the barn and brought out a team which they hitched to a wagon filled with seed wheat. The wagon was brought out to the middle of the yard. The two young men, with the help of Big Jake, pulled the two Van Brunt seed drills out of the shed. Jonas and Chris went back to the barn and brought out six more horses while Big Jake oiled all the bearings on the two seeding machines. They unhitched the two horses from the wagon to form part of a four-horse team for one of the drills. When both drills were ready, they drove the four-horse teams to positions on either side of the wagon loaded with wheat. Using large milk pails they dipped wheat from the wagon and filled both long boxes on the machines. Each box held ten bushels which would plant ten acres. They would fill them again at noon.

All day long the two teams marched back and forth across the fields. There was enough moisture in the rich, black soil, so that in a few days tiny green spears would begin to show in long straight rows in the little trenches formed by the revolving discs on the seeding machines. Jonas kept looking over the wide expanse of black soil and wondering if he would be around to see the thick velvet-green carpet of growing wheat that would cover the fields in a few weeks.

That evening at supper, Anna's happy questions drew responses from all but Big Jake. At noon, he had pleasantly answered her when she had prefaced her questions to him by calling him Papa. Tonight, though, he only grunted when spoken to, and stared at his plate, chewing his food. After supper the women began clearing the table and Big Jake reached in his pocket and pulled out a long envelope. "This was in the post office," he said, handing it to Jonas.

Jonas paled as he saw it. While he tore it open, Anna was at his side, a plate in her hand. She read the terse notice with him, unaware that the plate had fallen to the floor, breaking in half. She walked swiftly to the stairs, not wanting to break down before the family. Jonas stared after her and then followed, letter in hand. Elizabeth, knees buckling, sat down hard on a dining-room chair. The old haunted look returned to her face. Not looking directly at her, Big Jake said, "They give them two weeks before they have to go. The wheat should all be planted by then."

3

The two weeks passed swiftly, and Jonas was on the train for the first part of his journey to Camp Funston at Fort Riley. Several more young men boarded the train at Prairie Ridge. His cousin, Josh Zerger, took a seat beside him. Two other Mennonite men, a Wiens and a Thiessen from a Molotschna congregation took the seats across the aisle. A Burkholder and a Yoder, sat in front of them. They had boarded the train at Weaverton where there was a Pennsylvania Mennonite church. Three non-Mennonite men also got on and went to the back of the car.

Anna came with Jonas to the station, and would drive Blaze and the rig back home. Saying good-bye to his family had been hard. Everyone had followed to the rig and watched as he put his bag in the box behind the seat. Chris was closest, and he stuck out his hand awkwardly clasping Jonas's. "Take care," was all he could manage. The three girls stood in a row, each in turn shaking his hand, looking sad and perplexed. Elizabeth took his hand in both of hers, and, fighting back tears, said "Each day we'll pray the loving God will watch over you." Big Jake took Jonas's hand in his own big powerful one and squeezed so hard it hurt. Jonas could see his lips trembling as though he wanted to say something, but in a moment, he released his hand and stepped back.

Jumping into the rig beside Anna, Jonas issued a sharp command to Blaze. Moving quickly out the driveway, he looked back to see his family standing in a row watching after him. He waved. Glancing toward the big white house he realized that the coming night would be the first for him not under its roof.

In Prairie Ridge Jonas and Anna sat in the rig and watched while the train screamed, clanked, and hissed to a stop. When a man jumped out and put a little stool in front of the door of a car and yelled "Board," Jonas took Anna in his arms and gently kissed her. He didn't care if there was a crowd of people standing all around.

They had to change trains at McPherson. A large crowd waited on the platform. Most of the people were families of young men seeing them off to Fort Riley. A brass band played patriotic tunes. Some of the people sang along with the band and others tried to talk to one another, shouting above the music.

At the far end of the platform a small group of people waited, backs turned to the large, boisterous crowd. The Mennonite men from Prairie Ridge and Weaverton, clutching their duffel bags, made their way through the crowd and joined the small group at the far end, recognizing them as fellow Mennonites. Most were known to them, and introductions were made for those who were not. Some of the Mennonites waiting to see their young men off were older people who couldn't speak English, so the muted talk was in German. Since the Swiss couldn't understand the Plattdeutsch dialect of the Molotschna and Canton people, they spoke High German. Everyone crowded close so that their German speech would not be heard by the noisy crowd on the station platform.

Finally the train pulled into the station and the recruits, along with several uniformed soldiers returning from furloughs, were loaded into a car. The Mennonite draftees, because they were at the far end of the platform were told to enter the next car behind. When they entered, however, they were motioned to turn left and go to the next car. The result was that they found themselves in the back of the same car with the other recruits.

43

The train pulled out of the station, and Jonas occupied himself looking at the changing scenery. He had never been more than a few miles from home before, and had thought that all of Kansas was flat and covered with rich, black soil. The train was going through hilly land covered with grass. Where the land was plowed, the soil was light brown. On some of the hills there were stones sticking up out of the grass.

The dozen or more Mennonite men were either watching the landscape or talking quietly among themselves. The rest of the car, though, was very noisy. Jonas noticed several flasks being passed around. Some of the men were singing songs about saloon women and others were telling dirty jokes.

Jonas and his cousin Josh were sitting at the front of the Mennonite group. Directly across from them were two young boys who must have been twenty-one or they wouldn't have been there, but they looked more like seventeen. They were from the Canton community, members of the Holdeman Mennonite church. They both had the beginnings of whispy, blond beards on their delicate chins. Their shirts were obviously homemade, and their baggy trousers, held up by wide suspenders, looked homemade too. They held their wide-brimmed black hats on their laps. Their blond hair had recently been cut, probably by their fathers. Jonas had been told their names on the platform, but couldn't remember their first names. He remembered one was a Koehn and the other a Becker.

They had been sitting quietly looking out the window at the scenery. Suddenly one of the boys, pointing to a great herd of Hereford cattle grazing in the hills, said something excitedly in Low German. The loudest man in the car was sitting in the seat directly in front of the two boys. He had been drinking and had just announced for the third time to the whole car how many Huns he was going to kill "over there," when he overheard the Low German behind him. "Hey, men," he yelled, "look what we got here! A whole bunch of Christly Krauts." He turned around and spoke loudly to the two boys on the seat behind

44

him. "Hey, I hear tell you people all got pitchers o' Christ an' the Kaiser hangin' on your walls. 'Zat true?" Getting no response from the now terrified boys, he tried another tack. "Well anyhow, some o' your women look pretty good," he leered. His face flushed with alcohol, he leaned toward the two boys and, slurring his words, told them in obscene detail what he was going to do with "some o' them corn-fed Mennonite fillies" when he got out of "this man's army."

As the boys recoiled in horror, he laughed drunkenly, "Hell, you guys are all scared to fight. What could ya do 'cept stan' aroun' an' watch?" Some of the other men were becoming interested in the monologue and were watching and grinning.

The rage rising in Jonas threatened to choke him. Every instinct told him to leap at the man and smash his filthy mouth. His muscles tensed, and his knuckles whitened as he tightened his grip on the armrests. Josh put a hand on his forearm, and Jonas leaned back against the seat, still breathing hard. So this is what it means to be a Mennonite, a pacifist, a conscientious objector? The scum of the earth could spew their filth in your face and you had to sit still and take it!

The man looked around and saw he had an appreciative audience behind him. Turning again to the frightened boys, he opened his mouth to say more, but stopped and stared as the Friesen twins, Dave and Dan came up the aisle. They were identical twins, six feet, four inches tall and weighed about two hundred-twenty pounds, none of which was fat. The twin who was first in the aisle stopped beside the two boys, who by now were trembling and on the verge of tears. The big man leaned over and told them in Low German that they would like to trade seats with them. The boys, clutching their hats, ran to the back of the car while Dan and Dave settled comfortably into the vacated seats. Not caring to find out whether or not the two young giants were true pacifists, the would-be troublemaker turned around and stared straight ahead. In a little while he got up and made his way unsteadily to the other end of the car to the toilet. He must have found another seat at the far end of the car, for the Mennonite men didn't see him again.

At Junction City the men knew they were nearing their destination. East of the town the train moved slowly through the valley. The tracks lay between the Republican River and the rock-strewn, grass-covered hills paralleling it on the north. Soon after passing the historic stone ruins of the old territorial capitol of Kansas, the train coasted to a stop. They were in Camp Funston, a cluster of wooden buildings in the southeast corner of the sprawling military base called Fort Riley.

Men in uniform met the train and escorted the recruits to their barracks. The Mennonites were identified, separated from the rest, and taken to barracks number 527. As they approached the large unpainted two-storied structure, a double line of men was moving out of one end of it toward a one-story building they learned later was a mess hall. The soldier escorting them took them to the second floor where he told them to each pick a bunk, dump their bags on it, and follow him to the mess hall. He pointed to one of the lines of men waiting with trays in their hands, and told them to get in line.

Holding a tin tray, Jonas looked over the long tables with benches on either side filled with men eating supper from tin plates. He recognized at least a dozen men from around Prairie Ridge. After food had been put on their trays, he and Josh found a place across the table from two relatives from back home. From them they learned that barracks 527 was reserved for conscientious objectors. They were, as much as possible, kept separate from the regular army recruits.

"At first, when there were only a few of us," they said, "we had to sleep in the same barracks with the regulars. Things were pretty rough. We were beaten up on a pretty regular basis. Sometimes there were officers around, but they would just turn their backs and pretend nothing was happening."

Jonas was awakened before daylight the next morning by an incoherent bellowing on the floor below. As he lay listening, he realized the bellowing was an army man letting the men in the barracks know it was time to get up. The bellowing continued nonstop through the length of the building. Now the human noise machine was clomping up the plank stairs at one end of the building. Jonas watched as the khaki clad form reached the top of the stairs, bellowing as he came. About five feet, four or five inches tall, his body had the size and contours of a fifty-gallon oil drum.

"All right you Kaiser-lovin', sauerkraut-eatin' conchies, out of the sack! Get those plowboy feet on the floor! Now!"

Jonas slid out of his bunk and began putting on his clothes, unable to keep from staring at the man. He marveled at his blacksmith-bellows lungs that enabled him to shout out his obscenities for more than a full minute before he had to stop to take a breath. A split second was required to refill his lungs, and he was off again with his imaginative tirade. Jonas watched as his short legs propelled him the length of the long barracks to the stairs at the other end, bellowing all the way.

The newcomers were told that this was the way they started each day. Sergeant Kelly, secretly called *der Mundt*° by the men, came through the barracks at five-thirty each morning. At six the men lined up beside the barracks for roll call. The sergeant bellowed out each name in alphabetical sequence. Not bothering to learn the correct pronounciation of many of the more difficult German names, he pronounced them the way he thought they should be pronounced, with sometimes amusing results. The men soon learned his version of their names and responded when their names were called. Many of them, instead of saying "here," used the German word *hier*. The sergeant, however, was used to talking, not listening, so he didn't notice the difference.

After roll call the sergeant bellowed out the order that all those who had arrived the day before were to report to a building, which he pointed out, where they were to be examined and processed.

° The mouth.

By early afternoon all the men who had arrived the day before had been given a cursory physical examination, and were told to line up in rows along one side of the building. After a speech by an officer wearing a lot of medals and insignia , the men were formally inducted into the army. They were then directed to the quartermaster building where they were issued work uniforms.

Several hundred young men were standing around in a large room in the quartermaster building feeling self-conscious in their new, mostly ill-fitting uniforms. Many started conversations, pretending they weren't apprehensive, and so helped put one another at ease.

Suddenly Sergeant Kelly appeared. "Shaddup!" he bellowed to the room in general. Instantly quiet, the men moved back, giving him half the floor. He stood facing the newly uniformed men with his incongruously large feet spaced far apart. He was holding a sheet of paper before him which he studied intently, his wide lips moving as he silently read. He held his sergeant's cap under one arm, his orange-red hair, clipped close on the sides, standing straight up to a height of three inches on top of his head. His heavy jaws were partly obscured by the collar of his uniform. He had no neck.

The men stood staring at him uneasily until he finished going over what they soon realized was a list of names. "The following recruits will, as I read their names, step to the other side of the room," he bellowed, indicating the space on his left. After the second or third name was called, Jonas realized he was separating the conscientious objectors from the rest of the group. The names called were all Mennonite names. When the more than twenty Mennonite men were separated from the main group, the sergeant bellowed, "All right, you kraut-eatin' conchies, follow me. The rest of you men stay here. You'll be gettin' your orders in a few minutes."

With surprising speed for a man with such short legs, Kelly led the Mennonite men across the grounds to where a work crew was laying a cement walk between two widely spaced buildings. As they approached, Jonas recognized some of the men at work. Sergeant Kelly, who had been silent during the walk, now said, "Okay, clodhoppers, you can join your plowboy buddies. They'll tell ya what to do."

For the rest of the day Jonas and the other newcomers helped the work crew mix and lay cement. They mixed the cement by hand with garden hoes in large mortar boxes, then loaded it into wheelbarrows and dumped it between forms that had been laid out. The pliable cement was periodically leveled and troweled.

Having already laid several sidewalks at the camp, the Mennonites had convinced the officers of their knowledge of this type of construction work, and were not now being supervised by military personnel. Thus they could talk freely among themselves as they worked. The newcomers learned much about the army base and how to conduct themselves to stay out of trouble in a hostile environment.

The main buildings of the large military base were in the valley formed by the Kansas and the Republican Rivers running parallel for several miles before converging just south of Camp Funston. The level land in the valley was used for the many buildings required for a military installation as well as large parade grounds which were in constant use as new recruits were trained to march in formation. Some distance north of the rivers, the flat land, with its rich soil, ends abruptly at the base of barren hills extending many miles to the north. It was in these hills that most of the training for combat was done.

As Jonas helped mix cement for the sidewalk, he could hear the distant explosion of artillery shells and the crackling of rifle and machine gun fire. All over the parade grounds were groups of men marching in formation being yelled at by sergeants.

Between two barracks buildings Jonas could see a group of about twenty men walking single file in a large circle. A sergeant stood in the middle of the circle watching them and occasionally yelling, "Hup, two three four, hup, two three four." This was usually followed by a volley of curses. The

49

men, completely silent, walked as though on a treadmill, eyes downcast. They were not in uniform, but were all dressed alike. They wore homemade, collarless flannel shirts, and baggy black trousers held up by wide suspenders. On their heads were flat, wide-brimmed black hats. Most of the men wore beards with the upper lip shaved.

Jonas asked who these men were, and why they were walking around in a circle like that. He was told they were Hutterites who refused to do any work that would help the war effort. Nor would they put on army uniforms. They were having a bad time of it and were being constantly mistreated.

Jonas had heard of the Hutterites. They had a common origin with the Swiss Mennonites, but believed that Christ taught that ownership of private property was wrong, so they lived in colonies and shared everything. They had lived in Russia for a long time near the Low German Mennonites, and in 1874, when the great Mennonite migration took place, the Hutterites came too, and settled in South Dakota where they now had a number of colonies. Each colony was a large farm with fifteen to twenty families. The land and everything on it belonged to the whole colony. Everyone worked together, ate all their meals together, and lived like one family.

It took the men another day to finish the sidewalk. As they worked, they could see the Hutterites being harassed again. Instead of walking single file in a circle, the sergeants had them walking abreast around the entire perimeter of the immense parade ground. Yelling and prodding them with the barrels of their rifles, the sergeants kept them moving at a near trot. Two sergeants took turns driving them like cattle. As one round was completed, the sergeant who had been resting, sitting on the ground with his back against a barracks wall, would jump up and take over from the one completing the round. Hour after hour the Hutterites were driven until some began to stumble and fall. Letting them lie where they fell, the sergeants continued the game until they were themselves too tired to continue, and disappeared around the corner of the barracks.

50

When the Hutterites who were still on their feet realized they were no longer being driven, they too dropped to the ground where they lay panting.

After the two sergeants disappeared, Jonas filled a pail of water and, taking a tin cup, told Josh to do the same. The two men ran with their pails to the group of Hutterites lying near the barracks where they had collapsed. Leaving one pail with them, they ran with the other around the large field, giving water to those who had fallen along the way.

When they returned with their empty pails, they were met by two military policemen who took them to a tent in Detention Camp Number One. They were charged with leaving their assigned work areas without permission.

The next morning they were taken before an officer who gave them a severe reprimand and told them they could be court-martialed for such a breach of discipline. Since this was their first offense, they would be let off with a warning. Addressing the military policemen who had brought them from the detention camp, the officer said, "I'm sure appropriate work can be found for these men today."

The MPs saluted and ushered the offenders from the room.

Sergeant Kelly was waiting for them outside. Grinning widely, he bellowed, "Follow me, men!" The two MPs turned and walked away.

Jonas and Josh followed the stocky sergeant, puzzled by his strange behavior. They had thought him capable of communicating only by bellowing or snarling. Now, as he walked ahead of them, he treated them to a monologue about the beautiful fall weather, and became almost lyrical as he called their attention to the wide river and the sun-drenched hills beyond.

Suddenly he ducked into a doorway and motioned them to follow. By the time the young men realized they were in a huge latrine, Sergeant Kelly had taken two toothbrushes out of his pocket, handing one to each man. Beaming at them so that his wide mouth seemed to split his cheeks, his small, malevolent eyes stared at them. Pretending jocular goodwill, he said,

"You know I've had my eye on you two men ever since you got here. Why the first time I saw you, I said to myself, now there are two men who are here because they realize our glorious country is at war with a terrible enemy, and they have dedicated themselves to doing what they can to defeat that enemy. I made a vow right then and there, that if there was ever anything I could do to help you patriotic lads in your untiring efforts to overcome the Hun, I would be very happy to do it. Today you have your chance to do your very best for God and country. Now there are about one hundred porcelain fixtures in this here room, and they have been allowed to get into a deplorable condition filth-wise. So I'm leaving this equipment with you," pointing to the toothbrushes, "and when I come back this evening, each of these porcelain fixtures will be gleamin' white. Now you know we can't win no war with dirty toilets. No siree! So remember, Uncle Sam is depending on you. I have every confidence you boys ain't going to disappoint me." As he turned to go he said, "You know, when I trust somebody like I trust you men, and they let me down, I get downright despondent. I know you men don't want your ol' Sarge to be despondent, do you?" He disappeared out the door chuckling to himself.

The main business of the military post was the training of recruits. The conscientious objectors were a nuisance the military people didn't quite know how to deal with. They were in the way, and until the War Department issued some clear directives, no one knew what they were supposed to do with them. As winter set in, fewer jobs were found for them. They could not be given jobs in the mess hall kitchens because KP (kitchen police) duty was traditionally reserved as a form of punishment for minor infractions of rules by regular military men. There was a large cavalry installation at Fort Riley, and the Mennonites, who were mostly farmers, would not have minded being assigned the job of keeping the large horse barns clean. They were not allowed to do this either, because handling horse manure was the cavalry's version of KP, and was reserved as a discipinary function for cavalry troops.

Day after day, following morning roll call and breakfast, the conscientious objectors stood around waiting for work assignments. A sergeant usually appeared and ordered them to go stand on the hill. The men then walked up the hill overlooking the buildings and drill fields, where they stood until noon watching the regular soldiers drill. Afternoons were the same.

The boredom of camp life was frequently broken as individual conscientious objectors were ordered to report to the chaplain or to particular officers who questioneded them at length about their beliefs and gave them lectures on patriotism. While these interviews relieved the boredom, the men feared them because they knew the purpose of the interrogations was to try to trip them up and make them appear inconsistent or insincere. Few of the men were very articulate in explaining or defending their pacifist beliefs and answered most questions by reiterating that they were Mennonites and had always believed that war was wrong.

Jonas always looked forward to Saturday evening. The regular routine among the military people was relaxed from Saturday evening until Monday morning. The conscientious objectors, left pretty much to themselves during this time, didn't feel like they were under constant surveillance. Several had harmonicas and after supper on Saturday played popular tunes and hymns. Everyone sang along with the familiar tunes. They were always careful to sing the English words.

The men conducted church services each Sunday morning. When the weather was mild they held their services in the open near the river. They organized themselves into a choir and many of the regular army men, attracted by the four-part-harmony singing, gathered nearby to listen.

Mennonite preachers frequently visited the camp on Sunday morning and there would be a sermon. When there was no preacher the men took turns reading from the Bible. Several quartets were formed and Jonas sang tenor with one of them.

Christmas came and went. The winter dragged on.

4

In January some of the Mennonite men began applying for furloughs. Some were given one-week furloughs right away and others were turned down and told to apply later. After several applications, Jonas was given a one-week furlough in March. He was notified on a Tuesday that he was to report the next morning to be signed out and be ready to board the train at ten o'clock.

He found a telephone and called Anna. It was hard to make themselves heard over the party line, but after shouting at one another for several minutes, Jonas knew Anna was going to meet him at the station in McPherson. After they finished talking and Anna hung up, Jonas listened as about a dozen more receivers were replaced. Soon all of Prairie Ridge would know he was coming home tomorrow.

Jonas was too excited to sleep that night and the next morning he was among the first at the place where the train was to pick up the furloughed men. A sizable crowd had gathered before the train finally appeared. Jonas grinned happily at the crowd of noisy, exuberant soldiers standing closely around him. In his happiness he felt a close kinship with them all. Here he was not a part of barracks 527. He was a part of a crowd of young men sharing the happiness of going home after a long ordeal. Glancing at his uniform he saw himself as even looking like everyone else, and no one looked at him as being different. He was borne along with the happiness of the moment.

Someone began singing a ribald song and everyone joined in. Jonas wished he knew the words so he could join the singing. Suddenly he was struck with a feeling of guilt. Not because he had wished he could sing this forbidden song, but because he suddenly realized what the difference was between himself and the others. These men were on furlough to visit their families for the last time before being shipped off to the horrors of war, and he was coming back to wait out the war at Camp Funston—bored, but safe, because he was, by accident of birth, a Mennonite. The thought troubled him, and he realized it was something he was going to have to think about. Being a Mennonite didn't make him any better than these men who now seemed to him to be his brothers. Was his taking advantage of the special privileges granted Mennonites a betrayal of these brothers? He would have to think about this, but for now, he wanted to think about Anna and home and the farm.

Early in the afternoon the train pulled into the station at McPherson. Jonas, head out the window, had been trying to catch sight of Anna and the rig. His heart began pounding when he saw her seated in their little rig watching the train come to a stop. As soon as he could, Jonas jumped from the train, and hurried toward her. He threw his bag into the box behind the seat and climbed in beside her. In spite of the excited anticipation, their greeting was shy and restrained. After five months apart they would have to get to know each other all over again.

It was a long drive from the county seat to the farm, and Jonas, wanting this time alone with Anna before seeing the family, held Blaze down to a slow, steady trot. Miles before reaching the farm, they began passing the farms of relatives who stood on their porches or in their yards and called out greetings to them as they passed.

At last the farm came into view. Jonas felt a lump in his throat as he took in the familiar sight. The big square, white house at the end of the long driveway seemed dwarfed by the large red barn standing well back from the house. The farmstead also included two granaries with sheds on either side for wagons, buggies, and farm tools. There was a small hog barn, a corncrib, and a small chicken house. All the farm buildings were red. A mulberry hedge planted along the west and north edges of the large farmyard acted as a winter windbreak. Tall cottonwood trees lined both sides of the long driveway. The stark, straight lines of the square house were softened by the ash and elm trees and lilac bushes planted near it.

Even before they turned into the driveway, Jonas and Anna saw the family come out of the house to stand in the yard to wait for them. As they came to a stop, Chris stepped forward and took hold of Blaze's bridle, indicating that he would take care of unhitching him. He grinned happily at Jonas. When Jonas jumped out of the rig his mother took his hand in hers and smiled broadly at him as the tears welled up and spilled over onto her cheeks. The lump in Jonas's throat prevented him from speaking. He hadn't realized how much he had missed her until he looked at her now. She looked younger than when he had left in the fall. She had gained weight and her eyes were no longer sunken and sad looking.

When Elizabeth let go his hand, Jonas held out his hand to Big Jake who took it and pumped it vigorously, his jaws working as though he wanted to say something, but didn't quite know how to form the words. When Jonas said, "Hello Papa," tears began to well up in Big Jake's eyes. Embarrassed by this show of emotion by his father, Jonas turned to his little sisters standing in a row waiting their turn to greet him. As he shook hands with each of them, he said, "You girls have grown taller while I was away." They giggled, not knowing what to say to this big brother who had been away so long, and now was back dressed in strange clothes.

Turning, he clasped hands with Chris, who, trying to hide his emotion, bobbed his head and said, "I'll take care of Blaze."

Anna took Jonas's arm and led him into the house. Big Jake, Elizabeth, and the girls followed. Inside, the table was set for supper and Elizabeth and Anna went to the kitchen to finish preparing for the meal. Jonas went immediately upstairs where he saw Anna had laid out a pair of overalls and a shirt for him. He slipped out of his uniform and hung it in the closet where it would stay until he had to go back. Dressed in a blue shirt and overalls, he looked at himself in the mirror and smiled happily. He was a farmer and the mirror told him he looked the way a farmer should.

At the supper table, the awkwardness of the initial greeting over with and the strange uniform put away, Jonas found himself the center of attention as everyone asked questions about life at Camp Funston. Remembering the absolute silence at meals in the past, he marveled at the way everyone took part in the conversation.

He had everyone laughing as he described Sergeant Kelly and his ridiculous antics, but he was careful not to mention the Hutterites and their ill treatment, nor his own involvement with them and his punishment for it. It felt so good to be at home surrounded by his happy family that he didn't want to inject a note of sadness into the occasion.

Jonas suddenly realized that since leaving the train that afternoon, he hadn't heard an English word. How good it was not to have to look over your shoulder to see if someone was near enough to have heard you when, without thinking, you had said something in German!

After everyone had finished eating, the women cleared the table and washed the dishes. Big Jake got out his pipe and filled it with his homegrown tobacco. As he held a kitchen match over it, noisily drawing the flame into the tobacco, great clouds of smoke began billowing about his head. Satisfied that it was burning well, he settled back to enjoy his smoke.

Chris was filling Jonas in on how the farm work had gone while he was away, when the women, finished with their work in the kitchen, joined the family in the dining room. All sat around the table in the glow of the lamp hanging from the ceiling. Anna pulled her chair close to Jonas.

The subject of Camp Funston exhausted, Big Jake, between

puffs on his pipe, his eyes crinkling with amusement, recalled several practical jokes his cousin Pete and he had recently played on one another. Elizabeth spoke of pleasant visits she had had with relatives during the winter, and the little girls each told of experiences in school and Sunday school.

Suddenly Big Jake noticed that Jonas and Anna were no longer listening to the conversation, but were aware only of each other. "It's time for bed," he said to the girls. When they left the room he emptied his pipe, yawned elaborately and stood up. "It's been a long day, I think I'll go to bed too," he said, looking at Elizabeth. She got up to follow him. Chris, happy for the chance to visit with his long absent brother, began asking him a question, but a silent gesture from his father caught him in mid-sentence. He finished lamely with "Well, I guess it's bedtime," and hurriedly left the room.

Aware that they were alone, Jonas and Anna wordlessly got up and walked up the stairs to their room. The pleasure they found in each other that night was in sharp contrast to the terrible loneliness they had suffered in the previous months. Lying in each other's arms, they talked long into the night.

The days and nights went all too quickly. Everyone kept busy, but the farm work in March is usually not too pressing. One day they planted early potatoes and Jonas felt a deep sense of satisfaction working with the moist, black soil. The oats had been planted during the last week of February, and the wide, pale green spears were already two inches tall in the warm March sun. The corn would not be planted until all danger of frost was past after the first of April.

After the morning service on Sunday, everyone stopped to talk to Jonas and Anna. When they got home they saw Grossvatter's drozhki in the yard. Jonas loved his old grandparents and was always glad when they came for Sunday dinner.

By the time the women had finished with the dishes after dinner, the yard began filling up with buggies and automobiles. Within an hour there were about a hundred relatives in the house and yard.

Jonas was not surprised at all the attention he was getting. Sunday afternoon was the time for visiting. No special occasion was required for visiting, but when one occurred, it provided a focal point.

Anticipating the invasion of relatives, Anna and Elizabeth had spent all day Saturday baking pies, cakes, rolls, and huge pans of cookies. The two-gallon coffeepot, used only for special occasions, was brought out and made ready. Anna, thinking it wouldn't be large enough, called her mother and told her to bring hers.

By chore time, the yard began to empty. Several of the women and girls who weren't needed at home for chores stayed behind to help clean up the house, and all went together to evening preaching.

The next day Jonas and Anna had dinner with Anna's family. After dinner they took a walk down to the creek to sit under their favorite cottonwood tree. The ground was not as warm and dry as it had been the last time, so they took a blanket along to sit on. The March sun had begun to warm the earth and the buffalo grass in the pasture was beginning to show the pale green of new growth. The creek was running swift and wide, and the water was almost at their feet as they sat facing it with their backs against the rough cottonwood bark. The March wind had subsided that day and was a warm, gentle breeze on their faces.

Camp Funston seemed a long way off, but both were conscious that this was their last full day together. Jonas had to report back Tuesday evening. Both, however, put it out of their minds, and sat contentedly, hands intertwined.

Jonas broke the silence with, "I can hardly believe the change that has come over my family. How did you do it? For the first time since I was little, Mama is happy. And Papa! He makes jokes and laughs at home now, not just with his friends in town. They are both like different people, and it's all because of you."

"Oh no," Anna remonstrated, "it wasn't just me. Well

maybe my being there as a new member of the family helped. I know both of them wanted things to be different, but didn't know how to start making things different. I wanted to help but didn't know how. I tried to talk at the table—you know how my family talks all the time—but your papa would sit there like a stone with his eyes on his plate, and your mama acted like she was afraid to talk.

"Well, two days after you left, I decided to go visit Grossmutter Schrag and ask for her help. She is so beautiful and wise! We had a nice long visit, and she told me many things. She said that we must never forget that the man is the head of the family, but that the woman is the family's heart. It was the good Lord's intention that the two should work together, and if the heart was not functioning properly, neither could the head.

"She said that maybe the Lord had made me a part of this family so that I could help to make it whole again. She said that your mama needed lots of love, and that I should, in some way, show her every day that I loved her. 'With Big Jake,' she said, 'it won't be so easy. You'll have to start slow, and every day tell him something that pleases him and makes him feel that you think he is important.' So she told me a lot about your papa so that I could say the right things to him and ask the right questions. It took quite a while, but by Christmastime your papa was talking and laughing at the table and telling funny stories and making the rest of us laugh. He and Mama Elizabeth talk together now about things that happened when they were young, and she sings now while she works. So you see it was Grossmutter Schrag that caused things to be different."

Jonas stared at Anna's profile during her long speech, and wondered how one so young and beautiful could be so wise and good. He took her in his arms and kissed her tenderly, overcome with love for this woman God had given him.

5

When Jonas got back to Camp Funston he learned that the War Department had finally decided what to do with the conscientious objectors who were willing to work for the army and wear the uniform. They were told they could work in the Quartermaster Corps, in the Medical Corps, or continue to do maintenance and yard work at the army installations.

Thinking about the options, Jonas decided he wasn't suited to becoming a medic, and the men in the Quartermaster Corps seemed to work inside all the time, so he decided to stay where he was, doing yard work. Now that spring was here, yard work was more like farming than anything else.

The Hutterites still refused to wear uniforms or do any work, and were having a hard time of it. Working on the grounds, Jonas witnessed many incidents of harassment. One day a group of soldiers carrying rifles led a blindfolded Hutterite, with hands tied behind him, out of a detention tent and pushed him against a wall. One of the officers then pretended to read an order that he was to be shot for disobeying an order. He then called out to the men "Ready!" and the cocking of rifles could be heard. "Aim—fire!" A soldier then clapped two boards together. The tormented man's knees buckled. He remained in that position for several minutes while the soldiers laughed uproarously. They finally removed his blindfold, unbound his hands, and ordered him back to the detention tent. As he walked, uniformed men took turns kicking him.

One day while Jonas was pulling weeds near the shower room, he heard yelling and boisterous laughter coming from inside. A window was thrown open, and, one after another, six Hutterites, their clothing drenched, were thrown out the window. Before any could get up, their tormentors were upon them and began pulling them about by their legs, and some by the hair. Other uniformed men kicked them as they were being dragged about. Someone brought a scissors and the Hutterites offered no resistance as their hair and beards were cut in such a way as to make them look ridiculous.

Jonas was torn between outrage and pity for the tormented men and impatience with them for not giving in a little. The Mennonites who agreed to work in the camps were looked on with contempt by the regular soldiers, but at least they weren't mistreated and abused physically like the Hutterites.

Jonas and Anna wrote letters once each week. In May, Anna wrote that she was sure she was with child. She was very happy about it. Jonas wrote back trying to express his own happiness. Both found it difficult to express their innermost feelings on paper, and their letters consisted mainly of concern for one another's health and a report of their day-to-day activities. They could have expressed themselves much better in German but were afraid to write in German, believing that their mail might be censored.

In spite of Anna's attempts to write cheerful letters, they tended to depress Jonas, for they only served to accentuate his loneliness, and remind him that his real life was with Anna on the farm, instead of pulling weeds, mowing lawns, and watching men being yelled at as they were taught to march in formation in silly patterns around a field.

In June an order came through stating that all conscientious objectors refusing to work or wear a uniform were to be given farm furloughs. They were not to be furloughed to their home communities, however, but were to be sent to farms at least thirty miles from their homes. Handed down in June, the order was not implemented until August. While this reduced the

62

number of Hutterites at Camp Funston, it did not completely eliminate the problem. All newly drafted Hutterites were still sent to the army camp and kept there until they proved that they could not be coerced into wearing the uniform and accept work assignments. Thus the harassment continued.

For a short time in August there were no Hutterites in camp, but toward the end of the month four newly drafted men arrived. They were given the usual treatment when they refused to put on uniforms and accept work assignments. After several days they were told they could no longer eat in the mess hall. They were given daily rations of bread, some uncooked beans, raw bacon, and some coffee, and were directed to a ravine about a quarter mile from the mess hall. The only utensils they were given were two pails. They improvised a makeshift cooking facility from materials scrounged from a nearby dump. They found some empty cans, and thus were able to cook their food. This continued from September through the middle of November, when they were put in the guardhouse for refusing to build a stone walk from their tent to the mess hall.

Jonas learned later that they were court-martialed and sentenced to five years at Leavenworth prison, where two Hutterite men had died earlier as a result of being tortured.

By early fall rumors were circulated every day that the surrender of the Germans would happen at any time. When, on the eleventh of November it was confirmed that an armistice had been signed, the entire fort erupted in celebration. The Mennonites stayed close to barracks 527 that evening. They were concerned that some of the draftees, under the influence of liquor, would be disappointed at having missed their chance to fight the Germans and would remember that some were at hand. This did not happen, however, and the Mennonites were left alone to celebrate in their own way.

By midnight the men in 527 were all in their bunks and the lights were out. Few slept because of the noise of the revelry throughout the camp and their own excitement over the prospect of going home.

63

Jonas lay on his back, hands under his head, staring at the dimly lit ceiling. For a long time he lay smiling, thinking of his homecoming, of Anna, and how soft and warm she was in his arms. He thought of the baby and hoped he would be at home before it was born. In August Anna had written that Big Jake bought the Atkins quarter section, and the little house would be fixed up for them as soon as Jonas came home. There were so many plans to make! He and Anna would be in their own house. He would no longer be just Big Jake Schrag's boy. He would be Jonas Schrag, head of his own household! He grinned in the dark.

Images filled his mind, and for a time he held a picture of himself plowing the land on the Atkins farm. Sea gulls followed in his wake, picking grubs and worms from the moist, black, freshly turned earth. He looked toward the little house as he plowed and saw Anna, skirt billowing in the wind, hanging baby clothes on the line. The sun shone on her golden hair as she turned and waved to him. Jonas sighed with pleasure.

Other images crowded in. Many times since March, when Jonas had waited with the others for the train and felt a brotherliness with the men milling around him, their faces, clear and sharp in detail, had intruded into his mind. Now that the war was over, who among them would be coming home? Which of the men whose faces he so clearly remembered were now buried in France or Belgium? Surely some of them were Christians and yet they willingly went off to war. Remembering the stock answer he had always given to interrogating officers, "I am a Mennonite and we don't believe in war and fighting," it seemed now, somehow, not to be enough.

Searching for an answer, Jonas fell into a troubled sleep and dreamed that he and Anna, with their baby, were watching through the kitchen window of the little house on their farm as columns of steel-helmeted soldiers marched in formation toward them across the fields. When the soldiers on command, dropped to one knee, aimed their weapons at the house, awaiting the command to fire, Jonas pushed Anna and the baby to the floor and picked up his rabbit gun. With a defiant yell he shattered the window with the gun barrel, his finger on the trigger. The sound of breaking glass woke him. He lay sweating and trembling.

In the morning he saw a broken whiskey bottle on the sidewalk outside his window where a celebrating soldier had, after emptying it, given a defiant yell as he threw it high in the air to land and shatter on the concrete walk.

All over America the eleventh of November in that year of 1918 was a day of celebration. The town of Brinton was no exception. As soon as the news of the armistice was heard, people began gathering on the main street in a festive mood. Farmers and ranchers brought their families to town in their wagons, buggies, and Fords. Many a bottle was opened and shared to celebrate the war's end. By midafternoon the townspeople had made a great pile of packing crates and other debris in the middle of the street and set it ablaze. People began dancing around the fire shouting Indian war whoops. Someone raided a garden for a scarecrow and, declaring it to be the Kaiser, threw it on the fire. The crowd roared its approval. Several men, with the collaboration of the undertaker, brought a coffin and placed it on a pair of sawhorses in the middle of the street, inviting "mourners" to file by and view the Kaiser. What they saw as they looked into the open casket was a dead skunk lying on its back, paws neatly crossed over its breast.

Many farmers brought their shotguns to town, firing them into the air until they exhausted the supply of shells at the hardware store. When the last of the shells were sold, the hardware owner remembered he had several cartons of firecrackers left over from the fourth of July. He brought them out and sold them. The saloon keeper had built up his inventory in anticipation of an end-of-the-war celebration, so there was an ample supply of spirits. Enthusiastic volunteers periodically fed the bonfire with "Kaiser" scarecrows, assorted trash, and worn-out rubber tires.

A number of the town's leading businessman, including the president of the bank, stood in a circle near the fire engaged in earnest conversation as they passed a bottle. The banker did most of the talking. Suddenly they appeared to have reached some sort of agreement and all walked purposefully toward their cars. The banker, with his Buick, led a five-car procession out of town to the north. The crowd, engrossed in celebration, took little notice.

About an hour later the five cars returned, the Buick still in the lead, and parked in the middle of the street near the fire. Big Jake Schrag was in the backseat of the Buick. The crowd turned its attention to the car and the men milling around it. One of the men opened a back door and Big Jake was pulled out. His broad-brimmed hat fell on the ground as he came through the door. He stood calmly, towering above the excited men around him. The crowd fell silent as they stared at the big bearded man, dressed in blue overalls and flannel shirt. Most didn't understand what was happening, but sensed an interesting drama was about to take place.

Some of the men who had brought Big Jake to town now began to push him to the front of the car. Standing between the car and the fire, he stared over the heads of the crowd. His full, heavy beard concealed his convulsively working jaw muscles, his only sign of nervousness.

The banker, Rutherford Hays Wilson, a tall, lean man of about forty, with a hawklike face and an ambition to run for Congress, stood on the running board of his Buick and began to make a speech. "Friends, neighbors, patriotic Americans all," he began. Minutes into the speech he had the crowd responding enthusiastically to his patriotic rhetoric. At the end of each sentence everyone cheered and applauded.

Injecting a note of sadness into his voice, he said, "Not everyone in the vicinity of our fair little city, however, shares our love for our great and glorious country. While we were, at great sacrifice, buying war bonds to support the cause of liberty, and our boys were over there giving their lives fighting

66

and defeating the vicious, barbaric Hun, making the world safe for democracy, there were those on our very doorstep whose loyalties were not our loyalties, whose goals were not our goals. I speak, of course, of the German aliens who, throughout the war, demonstrated their loyalty to our enemies by using the language of the enemy and teaching their sons it was wrong to fight for America!"

The crowd, already long aware of the lack of patriotism among the Mennonites, roared its anger.

Pointing dramatically at Big Jake, Wilson bellowed, "Here is one, who, even though he became rich as the result of the war, refused to buy war bonds!"

The voice of the crowd was an ugly snarl.

At the right moment Wilson raised his hands benignly over the heads of the people. "Friends, neighbors!" he admonished them, "we are not vindictive people! In fact, we here on the plains of Kansas are well known for our tolerance of others' foibles. That is why we have, on this auspicious day of victory for the cause of democracy, brought Mr. Schrag to town to give him the opportunity to demonstrate that his loyalties are not with the Kaiser and his hordes, but with the country that has given him land and riches: our own glorious United States of America! The members of our city council have decided that we will have a victory parade here on Main Street, and that Mr. Schrag will lead our parade carrying the American flag."

The people cheered and whooped with laughter.

"And after participating in this demonstration of patriotism, I am sure we will have no difficulty persuading Mr. Schrag to, even at this late date, do his patriotic duty by investing substantially in Liberty Bonds."

A man came running from the General Store carrying a flag attached to a staff. He thrust it at Big Jake, who, still staring stoically over the heads of the crowd, held his hands stiffly at his sides. The man kept pushing the flag at him and finally let it drop at his feet. Jostled from behind, Big Jake stepped forward to keep his balance. His foot came down on the staff.

Someone yelled, "He stepped on the American flag!"

The crowd reacted like a nest of angry hornets. Those nearest him began to pummel him with their fists and to kick him. Several spit in his face. He closed his eyes and moved his feet apart to brace himself. The people, now a mindless mob, swirled around him kicking, striking, and spitting. A voice yelled, "Hang the son-of-a-bitch!" Others took it up. A man, dressed like a cowboy, threw a rope over his head, drawing it tightly about his neck. Two men, holding the rope, pulled him forward just as a man with a gallon can of yellow paint turned it upside down over his head. Temporarily blinded by the paint, Big Jake stumbled as he was jerked along the gravel covered street. He managed to get his big red handkerchief out of his pocket and wipe the paint from his eyes.

The mob was now yelling a litany, "Hang the son-of-a-bitch, hang the son-of-a-bitch!" People trampled each other to get to him to kick him and spit on him. Brown tobacco juice streaked the yellow paint covering his hair, beard, and clothes.

The men pulling Big Jake kept jerking the rope to keep him off balance. He managed to get a hand between the rope and his throat so that he could breathe. Those kicking him and spitting on him saw his lips move but didn't know what he was saying. His *"Herr Jesus hilf mir,"*° was drowned out by the mob's screaming chant, "Hang the son-of-a-bitch."

When they reached the little wooden jail with the big elm tree in front, one of the men threw the end of the rope over the large limb which extended over the edge of the street. Immediately three or four men grabbed it and pulled. Others pushed Big Jake until he was directly under the limb. The excitement of the mob was now at fever pitch. "Pull! Pull! Pull!" they yelled at the men with the rope.

The blast of a double-barrel shotgun fired into the air from a few feet behind the men pulling on the rope almost deafened

---

° Lord Jesus, help me.

68

them. They turned and stared at Tom Richards as he replaced the shells in his powerful gun.

"You men drop that rope," Richards said, pointing the gun at the men. The crowd was instantly quiet. Richards owned a large ranch northwest of town and was president of the Anti-Horse-Thief Association. He was well-liked and respected. In the absence of any formal law enforcement officials in the community he was often called on to function as unofficial law enforcer and arbiter of disputes.

The men hesitated, but, one by one, let go of the rope. When it hung slack, Richards, still holding the gun on the men, loosened it, pulled it over Big Jake's head, and dropped it on the ground. "Now you boys have gone far enough," he said. "There ain't gonna be no hangin' today. I'm puttin' this man in the jail here an' anybody takin' him out will do it over my dead body. Ever' last one o' you here is my friend, but the law is the law. If we ain't got no law, we ain't got nothin'."

He walked backward to the little jail, pointed shotgun in one hand, pulling Big Jake along with the other. Still facing the crowd, he reached behind him, opened the steel-bar gate and pushed Big Jake inside. The crowd stared sullenly. A few growled in protest.

"Now I'm gonna sit inside with this man, an' my shotgun is gonna be pointed at that gate," Richards said. "I don't figure we're gonna hafta be in there too long, 'cause I'm countin' on the fact that some o' you people got sense enough to know we can't take the law in our own hands, an' will call the sheriff in Newton so he can come take this man to the county jail for protection. If he committed a crime the law will take care of it, not us." He backed through the open doorway and closed the heavy iron gate behind him.

The jail, unused for years, was kept as a landmark and symbol of frontier days. One of the oldest buildings in town, it was built of heavy timbers and thick boards. The only opening was the heavy gate made of iron bars. There were two stools in the 10-by-12-foot room. Richards placed one in the center, told

Big Jake to sit on it, and, placing the other one in a corner, sat facing the door, shotgun laid across his knees.

The angry crowd milled around the jail. People were uncertain about what should be done. A number of tobacco chewers, proud of their ability to spit great distances with accuracy, took turns at the iron gate, and drenched Big Jake with tobacco juice. Others vented their frustration by screaming obscenities at him.

Most, however, began to drift away to their homes, some, a little ashamed of having participated. When the sheriff arrived at sundown, there was only a small group still milling in the street before the jail. The people stared silently at the sheriff as they parted to let him through.

In a few minutes Richards and the sheriff, guns drawn, came out of the jail with Big Jake between them. A murmer of hatred went through the crowd as they watched the big man, covered with filth, walk to the sheriff's car and get in the back seat. Before getting in himself, the sheriff stood for a moment on the running-board looking around at the silent, sullen people. "What kind of animals live here in Brinton, anyway?" he asked.

He made a U-turn in the wide street, drove to the main intersection, and turned east toward Newton and the county jail.

On Friday of that week Jonas returned to the barracks after supper and stretched out on his bunk. As usual he was thinking of home and speculating on how soon he would be there. Someone tossed an envelope on his chest. It was a letter from Anna.

He quickly tore it open and began to read. After the first few lines he sat up, his mind reeling at what he read. He read the letter through a second time. It had been written the evening of the twelfth after Big Jake had been returned to his home with the information that he would be tried in a federal court under the espionage act for desecrating the American flag.

Jonas continued to sit staring at the letter, rereading parts of it. The thought of his father, always walking tall and proud, being dragged through the street with a rope around his neck, kicked and spit upon by a screaming mob was beyond comprehension. For a moment Jonas hated. With all his being he hated those people who did this to his father.

He read the letter again. He had heard of Tom Richards, a man as big as Big Jake. He knew that Richards always carried a gun in a holster hanging from a wide belt slung low on his hips. A man with a violent past, he was often quoted as saying he had never killed a man that didn't need killing. Jonas never dreamed he would ever thank God for Tom Richards. He had always thought men like Richards stood for everything he detested, yet now he was thanking God for Richards and his guns for saving his father's life.

Jonas continued to stare at the letter. What was it the banker had said? "Here is one, who, even though he became rich as a result of the war, refused to buy war bonds!" Jonas thought again of the Atkins farm bought with war-priced wheat. When he plowed its rich, black soil, would he think of the children of Belgium who died of starvation, and of the men who waited with him for the train, his brothers, who died in the trenches? Would he see their blood in the furrows as he plowed? His throat ached as he longed for the days when he had been able to say simply and with conviction, "I am a Mennonite, and we don't believe in war and killing."

Every day more conscripted men received their discharges. Jonas became more and more frustrated. When would he finally be allowed to go home? At last, on the eighteenth of December, his name appeared on a list of men who were to report to the administration building. After a mustering-out ceremony, he was finally given his discharge papers. He tried to call Anna, but the party line to the farm was out of order, so he identified himself to the woman at the switchboard in Prairie Ridge and asked if she would try to contact his family so someone would meet him at the train station. His bag already packed, he ran to join the men waiting beside the tracks for the train that would take them home.

Late that afternoon, as the train approached the station in Prairie Ridge, Jonas strained to see if someone was waiting for him. The train moved so slowly! Finally he caught sight of Blaze. Chris was in the rig, sitting hunched over in his fleece-lined coat, collar up, against the sharp north wind. By the time the train stopped, Jonas was at the door. Before it was completely opened, he jumped off and was running toward his rig. Chris's big round face was grinning at him from between the wings of his high collar. Jonas threw his canvas bag into the box in back and jumped in beside Chris. "How's Anna?" he asked as he pulled the buffalo robe over his knees.

"Oh, Anna's fine. When I left she said, 'You hurry now and bring Jonas home so he can meet his son Menno.'" He flicked the reins, and Blaze jumped forward into a fast trot. To Jonas's look of surprise and wonder, Chris said, "Yeah, born this morning at six o'clock. That kid has sure got a pair of lungs." Then he looked away, embarrassed by the tears that welled up in his brother's eyes and spilled over onto his cheeks.

~~~~~~~~~~~~~~~

Part Two

MENNO

1944-1945

~~~~~~~~~~~~~~~

6

Menno emptied three five-gallon cans of distillate into the fuel tank of the old 15-30 McCormack-Deering tractor. The yellowish-colored, smelly liquid began to run down the outside of the tank just as the last drops fell from the can spout into the funnel. Removing the funnel and screwing the cap back on the fuel tank, he removed the cap on the one-gallon auxiliary tank welded to the end of the larger tank, and checked the gas level. It was about three quarters full, so he put the cap back on.

The tractor could run on the cheaper distillate fuel, but when the engine was cold it had to be started with gasoline. After it was warm he would readjust the valves in the fuel lines and the engine would run on distillate.

Checking the oil level, he opened the top petcock on the side of the crankcase and saw, with satisfaction, oil running out. He removed the radiator cap. The water level was low. While Menno went to the well for a can of water, his brother Andy greased the bearings on the tractor and plow. Menno filled the radiator, replaced the cap, and took one last look over the tractor and plow. He noticed a hex nut on a rear-wheel lug was loose. Taking the big open-end wrench from the toolbox bolted to the side of the tractor frame, he applied all his strength and tightened the loose nut.

Satisfied that everything was ready to go, he turned on the valve under the fuel tank and adjusted the levers for the spark retard and gas. He jiggled the gear shift lever to make sure the transmission was in neutral, then went to the front of the big tractor and pushed in the crank to engage the crankshaft giving the crank a quick twirl. Three times around and the engine roared into life. Starting in third gear, engine at half speed, he drove through the yard. He turned to wave to Andy who was standing beside the fuel barrels with the grease gun in his hand. The polished moldboards caught the rays of the setting sun and reflected spots of moving light on the granary as they went by. The steel lugs on the big tractor wheels left their distinctive marks on the hard surface of the driveway.

Pushing down the throttle to bring the engine to full speed, Menno lumbered down the long driveway at about five miles per hour. He crossed the road and drove through the wheat stubble to the far side of the south quarter section. When he reached the wide strip of black land, which had been plowed during the day, he shifted into second gear for more power, turned the tractor parallel with the plowed land, and guided the right wheels into the furrow. Reaching behind him, he jerked the rope tied to the trip mechanism of the plow and to the seat of the tractor. The three shiny fourteen-inch plowshares bit into the black soil and another forty-two inch strip of plowed land was being added to that already turned over.

Farmers in Kansas learned long ago that the sooner the land was plowed after the wheat was harvested, the better the soil conditions were for reseeding the wheat in the fall. Thus, if at all possible, they kept the tractors going day and night through late July and into August until all the land that was to be replanted to wheat was plowed.

Few tractors in 1944 were equipped with batteries and lights, so the plowing at night was usually done in the dark. If there was no moon, the stars provided enough light for the plowman to distinguish between the yellow wheat stubble and the black earth. This was all that was necessary to keep the wheels of the tractor in the furrow. The level land, consistent soil texture, and long fields also helped to make plowing at night without artificial lights possible.

Menno liked to plow at night, not only because he didn't have to endure the hot Kansas sun bearing down on him, but because the world seemed so much more peaceful. On this first night of plowing it was completely dark about an hour after sunset. The moon didn't rise until well after midnight, and then it was only a thin crescent, providing very little light.

The three-inch-high, narrow, knifelike steel extentions bolted to the flat rims of the small front wheels bit into the soil at the bottom of the furrow, keeping the tractor on course with scarcely any attention required of the driver. It was only when Menno came to the ends of the field that he had to give his full attention to his work. To make the ends straight and neat, he had to pull the trip-rope, lifting the plow out of the ground at exactly the right moment, and at the same time turn the tractor sharply to avoid running into the hedge on the one end and the barbed wire fence at the other. Skill was also required to properly enter the furrow for the return trip. He pulled the trip-rope again at the right time to ensure that the ends of the field were plowed evenly.

Once the end was negotiated, Menno had twelve minutes alone with his thoughts until he came to the other end. When the stars were particularly bright, he observed the various formations, taking special note of the brightest stars. Wishing he knew more about the night sky, he often thought of finding a book on astronomy and studying the stars, but somehow, he never got around to it.

Tonight, though, his thoughts were mostly about the war, or more specifically, the draft. He was twenty-five, and had, up until now, been regularly deferred as an essential farm worker. Now that Andy was eighteen, the draft board had decided that the farm was not large enough to need two draft-age workers, and especially so because their father, Jonas, was still young enough to work full time. Every day, when Emil Klassen the mailman left the mail in the box at the end of the driveway, Menno expected a letter from the draft board with his classification changed to IV-E.

Several weeks before, he had received notice from the draft board that his classification was 1-A. He immediately sent for "form 47," filled it out, and sent it back. Form 47 had to be filled out by anyone wanting conscientious objector status. Menno was certain that, any day now, he would get his IV-E which would give him official status as a conscientious objector. He would soon thereafter be sent to Fort Leavenworth for his physical. After that he would be assigned to a Civilian Public Service camp somewhere.

Menno often thought, with gratitude, of the changed laws that would keep him from having to be a part of the military as his father had been in World War I. The irony in the situation was that, now that the laws were changed so that pacifists no longer had to serve in the military, many of the young Mennonite men had given up pacifism and were serving as regular recruits in the armed services. Some were even voluntarily enlisting.

It had been several years since Menno had entertained any doubts about his own position on the question of pacifism. When the war started in Europe in 1939, he had thought about it a great deal, knowing, as did everyone else, that America would eventually be drawn into it. He and his friends often talked about the historic Mennonite attitude toward war. For a long time he allowed himself to be pulled back and forth between a firm conviction that logic demanded he participate in stopping the evil that threatened the world, and a firm conviction that, to be a follower of Christ meant to take Christ's teaching on pacifism seriously. By the time America entered the war, he had resolved the problem for himself by concluding that faith and logic were not necessarily compatible, and that, as a Christian, he must follow the teachings of Christ.

Bill Krehbiel was the first member of Menno's congregation to accept full military service. Preacher John Kaufman and the deacons called a meeting of the membership to decide what the position of the church should be on the question. The members were divided between those who believed that Bill should be "disfellowshiped," and those believing it to be a matter of individual conscience. Preacher John, old now and soon to retire, gave a talk in which he gave all the reasons why Mennonites have always been conscientious objectors to war, and why he himself was totally opposed to supporting war for any reason. In the end, though, he said he could answer to God only for himself, and could not presume to act as another man's conscience. Everyone must answer to God after having done what he believed was right. Many disagreed, but when a vote was taken, it was decided that no one was to be "churched" for joining the army.

All night long the tractor droned back and forth across the field. Menno lost track of time until he became aware that the sky in the east was beginning to lighten. It was surprising to see how quickly the dawn advanced. Soon he could discern the outline of the farm buildings across the road. In a little while, making the turn on the west end of the field, Menno saw the very edge of the brilliant sun come over the horizon. By the time half a disc had appeared, it was too bright for him to look at directly. Dewdrops shone like diamonds on the wheat stubble. As he made the turn on the east end of the field, he saw the shadow of the tractor extending to the middle of the level, half-mile long field.

He looked toward the house and saw Andy and Jonas on their way to the barn with milk pails. Menno turned again at the end, stopped the tractor, and opened the cap on the fuel tank to measure the fuel with the long end-wrench from the toolbox. Estimating the fuel would last another two rounds, he made them, put the tractor in high gear, and headed for home. As he entered the driveway between the two rows of stately cottonwood trees he saw Jonas and Andy walking toward the house with foam-topped milk pails. The half-dozen red and white cows were making their way single file down the lane to the pasture.

As he passed the house, Menno reached under the fuel tank and closed the valve, timing it so the engine would stop by the time he got to the fuel barrels. He refueled the tractor and serviced it so that when Andy had finished breakfast, it would be ready to take out to the field again. A fast eater, Andy was out of the house and ready to go just as Menno finished.

"Good morning, Night Owl," he greeted Menno.

"Well, I was just doing what the Amish people always say, 'Plow deep while sluggards sleep.' "

Andy put a wet burlap-covered jug of drinking water on the tractor platform and was about to start when Menno stopped him with, "Hey, wait a minute. This is Saturday, so I'm not going to plow tonight. Why don't you bring it in about one o'clock this afternoon and we'll fill 'er up and I'll take over for a couple of hours, then you can plow again 'til dark."

"Okay, see you about one," Andy said as he gave the crank a quick turn, bringing the engine to life again.

Menno went to the house where the rest of the family was waiting to eat breakfast. He washed at the sink on the closed-in back porch, dried with the roller towel and stepped into the kitchen. His mother was standing over the eggs and sausage at the stove. "Well, good morning Night Owl," Anna said cheerfully, interrupting the hymn she was singing.

"Good morning. Boy, that sure smells good," he said as he passed into the dining room. He exchanged greetings with his sister Marie, almost bumping into her as they met at the doorway. She was taking Andy's dishes to the kitchen.

Jonas was sitting in his chair at the head of the table reading from a small Mennonite devotional book. When Menno came in Jonas laid the book down. "You must have turned over a lot of stubble. I woke up several times during the night and I could hear the old tractor roaring away."

"Yeah, it went pretty well. It only plugged up once, and it wouldn't have then if I had been able to see the pile of straw before I went through it."

Anna and Marie came in with the food and they all sat down. When all was ready Jonas asked the blessing. Among other things he asked that Kate and Martin be watched over.

Kate was the older of the two sisters and was two years younger than Menno. She had been married for several weeks to Martin Reimer from one of the Molotschna Mennonite churches. They were married just before he was drafted and sent to serve in a CPS camp near Colorado Springs. Kate, together with a friend of hers also married to a man in the same camp, rented a two-bedroom apartment in the town of Colorado Springs so they could be near their husbands.

After breakfast Menno went to the barn with Jonas to help him get the horses ready for the gangplow. Most of the farmers in the area had long ago disposed of their horses, although a few still kept a two-horse team to use occasionally for the odd job that could be done better with horses than with a tractor. Jonas, however, still kept four horses, and, especially at plowing time, used them just as in the old days.

When Menno was two years old, his grandparents, Big Jake and Elizabeth, moved to town and Jonas and Anna moved into the big house. The buildings on the former Atkins place were later dismantled, the lumber used to build a large granary. Jonas and his brother Chris formed a partnership, taking over the operation of the farm. One of the first things they did was buy a Fordson tractor. Chris took over the tractor work, and Jonas continued to work with horses. When Menno was nine, his uncle Chris got married and decided to quit farming and go into the farm machinery business. Jonas bought out his interest in the partnership. Big Jake still owned all the land and buildings.

Until Menno was fifteen or sixteen, and old enough to work all day on a tractor, Jonas hired one or another of Anna's younger brothers to run the tractor during the busy seasons. He still preferred to work with his horses.

No mares had been bred on the farm for more than fifteen years, so Jonas's four horses were all past their prime, but were still capable of a day's work if they weren't pushed. They enjoyed a good rest at each end of the field and were kept in the barn for two hours at noon. Jonas realized that the amount of plowing he was getting done, compared with what his sons were doing with the big tractor, was negligible, but he reasoned that they were doing what they liked best, and so was he, and that's what really mattered.

After Menno had helped Jonas hitch the horses to the old gangplow and saw them start for the field west of the barn, he went to his room to sleep until one o'clock. He woke up when he heard Andy drive to the fuel barrels to fill up. He went downstairs and had a quick snack before taking the tractor back to the field.

He was glad to see Andy come back to the field to take over the plowing soon after three o'clock. He wanted to do some work on his car before using it later in the evening. His '37 Ford was in pretty good shape mechanically, but the tires weren't very good. They were all recaps, and he had noticed a bulge on the side of one almost as big as a fist. He thought a boot and a liner would fix it, but it would take time.

He could only get an "A" ration card for gas for his car since it was the second car on the farm. An "A" card didn't entitle one to new tires. If he couldn't find any 600-16 size tire carcasses and get them recapped, he could always get his uncle Chris to sell him some sixteen-inch implement tires. They seemed to work on cars if they weren't driven over thirty miles per hour.

By the time Jonas brought his horses in from the field, Menno had the tire fixed. He helped his father with the horses, and together they did the evening chores. After supper Menno took a bath and changed clothes.

"I won't be out late," he said as he left the house. The sun was beginning to set as he started down the road in his old black Ford. He drove slowly until he got Andy's attention from out in the middle of the field. To make sure Andy could see him waving, he gave an exaggerated wave with his arm out the window and high above the car. *Andy's a good kid*, he thought to himself. *I just hope this stupid war is over before they come after him.*

82

It was a fifteen-minute drive to Rachel Kaufman's house. Menno and Rachel had been going together for over a year now. They liked to be together and Menno was beginning to think that maybe they were in love. Rachel had been sure for a long time. Menno liked her family, especially her mother and brothers and sisters. He wasn't sure how he felt about her father who was a little hard to figure out. He didn't talk much, and when he did, he seemed to express some pretty strange prejudices. He took himself seriously. Back in April of 1917 he had gone to Manitoba and hired out as a farm hand to an Old Colony Mennonite farmer. He left Canada on November 11, 1918, returning to the family farm in Kansas. He never mentioned his Canadian sojourn, but often expressed his contempt for Mennonites who in any way participated in the war effort in the first World War. His reaction to Mennonites joining the army in World War II was one of almost incoherent rage.

Rachel's mother opened the screen door for him when Menno knocked. She gave him a friendly greeting as did several brothers and sisters in the room. They were listening to Gabriel Heater's news broadcast. "There is good news tonight! United States Marines have established solid beachheads on Guam.... Bulletin! Just in from Europe.... Russian forces have overrun the Polish city of Lublin and are advancing on Lemberg!... You mothers praying for your sons tonight, know this ... the enemy is being brought to his knees!"

In a few minutes Rachel came down. Her mother, in a bantering tone said, "Now don't you two stay out so late you'll be sleepy in church tomorrow."

"Don't worry, mama, we won't be out late," Rachel said as they exchanged friendly good-byes with all in the room. Menno could see Rachel's father, Tobias, reading a paper in the next room. He didn't look up.

In the car Rachel said her friend Selma Jantz had called that day to tell her there was to be a "gathering" at her place that evening. The Ludwig Jantz farm was more than ten miles north in Lone Tree Township, and when Menno and Rachel arrived it was dark. The young people were all out in the yard square dancing in the light of Coleman lanterns hanging from tree limbs.

Parties and dancing were *verboten*° among the Mennonites, so the young people called their parties "gatherings," and square dancing was called "musical games" to escape the censure of their elders.

Menno parked the car with the others drawn up in a row outside the large fenced-in yard. As they came through the gate the music stopped and Hank Boese, who had been calling the dance, sat down. Everyone seemed to be talking at once. Suddenly there were whoops of laughter. Dave Unruh caught sight of Menno and Rachel and yelled, "Hey, Menno, get a load o' this. Helmut pinched Elsie and she said 'You stop that Helmut or I'll raise cain with you' "

Knowing Helmut's family name was Koehn, Menno laughed appreciatively.

"Hey, Helmut! I'll bet that's the best offer you had all day!" someone else called loudly to the embarrassed Helmut.

While everyone shouted above the music, two fiddles, two harmonicas, a guitar, and a banjo played "Arkansas Traveller" and "Who Broke the Lock on the Henhouse Door?" What the music lacked in quality was made up in speed and volume. *Plattdeutsch*, the Low German dialect, was usually mixed freely with English at these gatherings, but tonight, with deference to the several couples from the Swiss community who couldn't understand it very well, all conversation was in English.

When the next dance was called, Menno and Rachel allemanded and dos-à-doed with the rest. The gathering broke up about midnight after homemade ice cream and cake.

"See you in church!" everyone called to everyone else as they moved toward their cars.

° Forbidden.

7

Menno tossed restlessly as the bright square of sunlight from the open window crept over his pillow and began to penetrate his closed eyelids. Slowly he came awake. When he realized it was Sunday morning, he swung his feet to the floor, yawned, stretched, and dressed. Downstairs, he saw Anna preparing breakfast. Jonas and Andy were at the barn.

"Well, look at you," Anna said smiling, "all dressed up. You think the cows will recognize you?"

"Aw, I didn't think daddy and Andy would mind choring without me this morning. Rachel's cousin, Ruth Graber, invited us to dinner today, and we thought we'd go early and go to Sunday school and church at the Ninnescah Springs church. That way we could see all our Reno County relatives."

"That will be nice," Anna said as she went about her work. While Menno shaved at the mirror in the corner of the big kitchen, Anna named a long list of relatives to whom he was to give her regards.

It was a long drive to Ninnescah Springs, so Menno ate a quick breakfast and hurried to his car just as Jonas and Andy came in from the barn. He checked the oil level and gas gauge and gave each tire a kick, checking for bulges.

Rachel was waiting for him when he drove into the Kaufman yard and met him at the car before he had a chance to go to the door for her. Swinging out the driveway they drove south over the smooth, hard-packed dirt road. As they passed farm after farm Menno checked to see how much plowing had been done. When they arrived at the big Mennonite church east of Ninnescah Springs, they saw that the parking lot was full of cars. The opening exercises for Sunday school had just started. The Swiss church here was larger than Menno's church in Prairie Ridge, but not as large as the congregation Rachel belonged to west of Prairie Ridge. When the Swiss Mennonites came from Russia to Kansas in 1874, the more than four hundred people were all members of one congregation. By 1944, they had multiplied to several thousand. Having spread out over a large area, they were now organized into six separate congregations.

The congregation settled down for the worship service following Sunday school. After the usual singing of hymns, Scripture reading, and prayer, the pastor, a young man who had studied in the East, began his sermon, entitled "The Christian's Response to War." Menno listened, spellbound, as the preacher carefully articulated all the reasons why a Christian should not participate in war. He cited, of course, the teaching of Christ and the examples set by him and the apostles. He spoke of political morality and gospel morality, and that the two are often diametrically opposed. While the Christian should be ready to "render unto Caesar the things that are Caesar's," he must at all times be ready to obey the laws of God rather than the laws of man.

While the laws of civilized nations are generally based on the laws of God, in times of war nations put a moratorium on the ethical and demand that citizens obey the laws of a sovereign state rather than the laws of a sovereign God.

Summing up, he said, "What then must faithful Christians do when the state would constrain them to commit an act they consider a denial of Jesus Christ? Their submission to the state can then only be a false witness. When the state violates God's law, the church would be unfaithful to its own ministry and its responsibility toward the state if it did not clearly protest. This protest can be embodied in definite and significant acts. Christians, however, must patiently endure, without rebellion, the injustices of which they may themselves be the victims at the hands of the state.

"When the state violates the laws of God and tries to make Christians take a personal part in such violation, the child of God must respectfully but openly disobey that demand by the state. This is the price of being a committed disciple of Jesus Christ."

The service closed with the congregation singing "Faith of our Fathers," followed by the benediction.

After the service and the visiting outside, Menno and Rachel followed the Graber car to their farm several miles south and east of the church. One of the subjects discussed at the dinner table was life in the CPS camps. The Grabers' oldest son was serving in the Civilian Public Service in Colorado. He wrote home regularly, telling his family of his activities. They had planted trees in the spring, and were now building and maintaining roads in the national forests. Some of them were doubling as forest rangers, and it seems all of them were being trained to fight forest fires.

After dinner the men visited on the front porch while the women cleaned up the dishes. Just as the women came out to join the men, two carloads of young people from the church drove in. The young people all moved out into the shady yard and sat in a circle on the Bermuda grass under a huge elm tree.

Most were in a talkative mood and for a time the conversation was light and bantering. Two of the young women were engaged to Mennonite men who had decided against pacifism and were now in Europe. Most were therefore reluctant to speak about that which was uppermost in their minds—the war. Finally, during a lull in the conversation Pete Zerger turned to Menno and asked, "What did you think of the sermon this morning?"

"I guess I go along with everything he said," Menno said, glancing at Ruth and Linda Graber whose boy friends were in Europe. He didn't want to offend.

"I thought it was fantastic," Dave Krehbiel interjected. Dave, a religion major at the Mennonite college in Newton, was 4-F because of a childhood leg injury which had left him with a permanent limp. "He went right down the line and explained what it's all about. There's no other way a Christian can possibly look at war."

"Doesn't every coin have two sides?" Ruth Graber asked quietly.

"Oh absolutely," Dave said, pleased at the prospect of dialogue. "True Christianity has always been dualistic, seeing everything in terms of polarities—good and evil, light and darkness, the kingdom of God and the kingdoms of this world. Everything has its opposite. Our ancestors declared themselves to be citizens of the kingdom of God and believed themselves to be compelled to live by its rules and not those of the kingdoms of this world."

"If you're talking about the sixteenth-century Swiss Anabaptists," Ruth protested, "they lived in a different world than we do. The issues they faced were not the same as ours. Our world is much more complex."

"Oh, but the issues are the same!" Dave was becoming excited. "It was then as now a question of allegiance, and their allegiance was to Jesus Christ, just where ours should be. They saw things, not in the perspective of political and sociological history as we do in this secular age, but they looked at the world with a cosmic overview, and if we looked at things from that perspective, we'd come to the same conclusions they did. Four hundred years from now the political issues of this war will seem pretty remote. The kingdoms of this world are transient and not worthy of our total allegiance. The issues facing the sixteenth-century Anabaptists in Switzerland were qualitatively the same as those we face now."

"I think you attribute insights to our ancestors they didn't have," Ruth protested.

"On the contrary, it is we modern-day Mennonites who have, to a large extent, lost the vision our forefathers had.

We've compromised with the world so much in order to gain special privileges that we've lost sight of why we are pacifists in the first place." Thinking a moment, he said, "Not all of us though. I keep thinking of the two Hutterites martyred in Fort Leavenworth in 1918. Just as our sixteenth-century ancestors were totally committed to their principles, those Hutterites were willing to give up their lives for the faith."

"Speaking of the Hutterites," Pete Zerger broke in, "I think it would be a lot easier for us if our churches took a hard line on pacifism like the Hutterites do and told us exactly what we should do. That way we'd know everyone was 100 percent behind us and we'd have no doubts that what we're doing is right."

Several of the young people shook their heads in disagreement, and Dave said, "Hey, you want it to be too easy. Sure, Mennonites have always been known for their doctrine of nonresistance, but if we take that doctrine along with other things we believe and engrave them in tablets of stone, we're in trouble. What sets us apart from authoritarian and legalistic churches even more than our pacifism is the idea of the priesthood of the believer. If you are your own priest, responsible only to God, I can't presume to tell you what God's will is for your life. All I can do is encourage you to search it out yourself and if, after an honest search, you disagree with me on the subject of pacifism, or anything else for that matter, I have no right to condemn you."

"Sort of like 'I disagree with what you say, but will defend to the death your right to say it,' " Pete grinned.

"Exactly," Dave said.

Ruth laughed. "Can't you just see Dave out there slashing away with his trusty sword, defending to the death the right of free speech!"

"Yeah," Dave chuckled, "I guess 'Defend to the death' sort of conjures up the wrong image for us defenseless Mennonites."

"Well I don't know, Dave," Rachel spoke up, "when you

89

really get going about something you really believe in, I think a slashing sword is a pretty good image."

"I guess you're right. I do sort of get carried away."

The conversation drifted to lighter subjects, and about five-thirty, after cookies and coffee, the visitors began to leave. At the car Ruth hugged Rachel. "Hey you two, let's do this again soon."

"Sure," Menno said. "This was great. I really enjoyed it."

The road home for Menno and Rachel went through Hutchinson. On the wide main street they saw an open restaurant and decided to stop for a snack. Getting out of the car, Menno joked, "I'm glad there are some heathen here in 'Hutch.' If the town was solid Mennonite, they'd let us starve on Sunday."

Inside there were booths along both sidewalls and a row of tables down the middle. A counter with stools ran along the back wall. The kitchen was beyond the counter behind a large opening in the wall through which the food was passed to the dining room. The cash register was on one end of the counter.

Menno and Rachel chose a booth about midway down on the right side. The restaurant had few customers. In a booth directly across from them were two high school couples sipping cokes. The girls typically wore their hair pageboy style. Their blouses had puffed sleeves and their skirts were tight and short. They wore white bobby-sox and penny loafers. The boys wore loose-fitting, pleated trousers and striped, well-ironed shirts. Their hair, clipped short on the sides and back, was glistening with Brilliantine.

While the waitress, another high school girl dressed like the two in the booth, took Menno and Rachel's order of hamburgers and Cokes, one of the boys in the booth went to the jukebox in the corner and put in a coin. Before he got back to the booth, the machine was loudly playing the popular song, "Praise the Lord and Pass the Ammunition."

Just as the nickel's worth of music came to an end, the other customers, two middle-aged women dressed in their Sunday finery, got up from their table and went to the cash register. They paid their bill and started to walk out, but stopped at Menno and Rachel's booth. Menno, his back toward the cash register, didn't notice their approach, and was just putting his water glass to his lips, when one of the women snapped, "Young man, why aren't you in uniform?"

Menno choked on the water, and in the ensuing coughing fit, the two righteous ladies stalked out of the restaurant. When Menno finally recovered, he looked at Rachel as if to say, "How do you react to something like that?"

Rachel patted his hand. "Don't worry about it," she said. "They probably heard a sermon this morning on Christian patriotism and were still feeling very Christian and very patriotic."

The girl brought their hamburgers and Cokes. They silently munched and sipped. The kids in the booth didn't have any more nickles for music and soon left, driving away in a model "A" Ford.

Rachel broke the silence. "Dave sure was wound up today. What did you think about what he had to say?"

Menno chewed his burger. "Well, you know how these college kids are—have everything all figured out and then snow everybody under with words."

"I sure agreed with everything he said, though."

"Yeah, well—I guess it makes everything a lot easier if you believe so strong that you don't even have to think about the other fellow's point of view."

Rachel tensed. "But how can we not believe that war is wrong?"

"You know, that's exactly what I asked Bill Krehbiel when he was home on furlough last month. He said he never doubted for a minute that war was wrong, but that it just wasn't that simple. 'Okay,' he said, 'here we are, a small minority who say that it is against our conscience to fight because we must love our enemies, so the majority says they have to fight to protect pacifists so that they can have the right to think as they do, so then the majority, the nonbelievers, die so that the minority, the believers, may live. So who is the martyr for the faith?' "

"Ach Menno, you scare me when you talk like that. This afternoon when you told Dave you agreed with what the preacher said this morning I thought that you had gotten rid of your doubts."

"Well, most of the time I'm okay, but sometimes I just can't help but see the other side—like when I hear some of our pious relatives condemning those who've gone into the army and all the while they themselves are raking in money producing food for the army. Sometimes I get so confused. I wish God would come down and say 'This is the way.' "

"Haven't we always been taught that he did?"

A slow grin spread over Menno's face. "Did anyone ever tell you that you have a knack for saying the right thing at the right time?"

Both were moody and silent as they continued the trip home. Rachel pressed against Menno as he drove north out of town. He put his arm around her and together they watched the sun, now a great orange disc, slowly disappear over the straight-line horizon.

8

Menno and Andy kept the tractor going constantly between Monday mornings and Saturday nights, and had the four-hundred acres plowed by the middle of August. During that time Menno received confirmation of his conscientious objector status. Then, in early September he received his notice to report to Fort Leavenworth for his physical. He had ten days, which included two weekends, before having to report to the county court house for transportation to the induction center.

Calling Rachel at noon on the second Saturday, he suggested they have supper at a restaurant in Newton and then see a movie. He picked her up about six o'clock and they were in Newton before seven. They decided to eat at the Harvey House. Just as they began their meal, two men in military uniforms, accompanied by two young women, came in and took a table near them. They didn't recognize the women, but the two men, Dick Harris and Dave Gering, cousins to each other, were relatives of both Menno and Rachel. They nodded greetings, but didn't introduce their companions.

The two couples had apparently been drinking before coming into the restaurant. The two women and Dick Harris spoke too loudly. Dave Gering, aware that many of the customers at the tables were Mennonites, and some of them relatives, was acutely embarrassed and stared silently at the table.

Ordering for the four of them when the waiter appeared at their table, Dick acted belligerently toward the black man, calling him "boy" several times, even though the man was obviously in his forties.

When the waiter left to place their order, Dick continued in a loud voice, "Like I was sayin', shootin' down those Nazi pigs can really get excitin'. Did I tell ya I got ten of 'em? Can't wait to get back over there an' get at it again!" Pretending he was holding on to an airforce machine gun, he swung the imaginary weapon in a wide arc, jerking his entire body in unison with his loud "ack, ack, ack, ack, ack!"

Becoming aware that conversation at the other tables had ceased, he was encouraged to go on. "Man, you should see them when they get hit! Sometimes they start to burn right away an' by the time they hit good ol' mother earth, there ain't nothin' left but scorched tin, but sometimes they just go down. Man, I wonder what those Nazi pigs are thinkin' about on the way down," he chuckled. Holding his hand high above his head, he pointed toward the floor and began a slow, downward spiral. Attempting to simulate the sound of the falling plane, he continued the spiral motion until his extended finger struck the floor beside his chair. "Va-Whoom," he jerked his body up and backward, pretending to have been blown backward by the explosion. "Another crew of Nazi swine have just become good Nazis. You know the ol' sayin', the only good Nazi is a dead Nazi!"

Miserably embarrassed, Dave sat with his elbows on the table, his chin resting on the heels of his palms, his hands shielding the sides of his face.

Menno and Rachel ate quickly, the food tasteless, so they could leave. The waiter brought the order for Dick and his table and was again abused for his trouble. The food, however, absorbed Dick's full attention for a few minutes, but he soon continued his monologue between mouthfuls.

Menno finished eating, and Rachel said, "Why don't you ask for the check? I'll be finished in a minute."

Catching Menno's signal, the waiter approached their table. "Dessert, sir?" he asked.

"No thank you, we'd like our check please."

As the waiter stepped back to write up the bill, Dick called over, "How's my ol' buddy Menno? Long time no see. I see you're still not in uniform. Oh yeah, I forgot. You're one o' them con-she-an-shus ob-ject-ors," he snickered, sounding each syllable to show his contempt. "Well, I'll be thinkin' of you plantin' them little trees or emptyin' bedpans while I'm over there doin' a man's job." As an afterthought, he said, "Or are they gonna let you stay down on the farm so you can keep on milkin' them cows an' spreadin' all that manure?" He looked around to reassure himself of his audience. The two women giggled. He looked at them appreciatively.

From the time the food arrived, Dave had not looked up from his plate.

Pale with anger, his jaw muscles working comvulsively, Menno picked up the check and, with Rachel, walked to the cash register. Dick watched him go, his face revealing his hatred. "These holy, self-righteous, mealymouthed, hypocritical Mennonites are goin' to hear more from me yet before it's over with. I'm sittin' in the catbird seat now, and I'll never have to take any crap from them again," he said vindictively.

Paying the bill to the manager at the cash register, Menno could see his undisguised smirk. The man had apparently enjoyed the little drama in which the conscientious objectors were put down by one of their own relatives.

What kind of a man, Menno thought in silent, compressed anger, *would let someone like a drunk Dick Harris come in here and spit on the beliefs of his mother and his community, and think, as he obviously does, that it's patriotism?*

Out in the car, still pale with anger, Menno sat behind the wheel and gripped it so hard his knuckles were white. "I've never before in my life wanted to smash somebody's face so bad," he said between clenched teeth.

Rachel put her hand on his shoulder. "Menno, you're trembling. Why did you let him get to you this way? Remember what he is. Don't be angry with him. Pity him."

His anger receding, Menno recalled Dick Harris' story.

Years ago, Joe Harris had come to Prairie Ridge from one of the Southern states to work in the wheat harvest. Staying on after harvest, he got a job on the railroad as a section hand. He learned to know Hannah Graber while working in the harvest for her father, and within several months they wanted to be married. Her parents were opposed to the idea until she convinced Joe to join her church. After several sessions of individual instruction from Preacher John, he joined. Several weeks later they were married. Joe never felt at ease among his wife's many relatives and within a few months he stopped attending services.

Dick was the oldest of their three children, and the only boy. When he was about five or six, his father became chronically ill and could no longer work. The burden of providing for the three children and their sick father fell on Hannah's frail shoulders. Relatives helped, but Joe, bitter over being unable to provide for his family, often became abusive to his wife's well-meaning relatives when they brought used clothing or food to their little rented house at the edge of town beside the railroad tracks. He became more and more withdrawn. Finally becoming completely catatonic, he had to be sent to the state hospital at Larned. He died there several years later.

The wives of several businessmen in town hired Hannah, on a regular basis, one day a week to clean their large houses. She maintained a large garden behind her little house, and relatives continued to supply the family with clothing their own children had outgrown.

When Dick was about ten, his mother was no longer able to make him go to Sunday school and church with her and his sisters. He had seen another boy grin at him as he recognized the clothes Dick was wearing as his own cast-offs. He was never seen in church again.

He began haunting the grocery stores for the chance to earn a few nickels and dimes making deliveries. He mowed lawns and cleaned basements. Carefully saving his nickels, dimes, and quarters, he was able to buy his own clothes. Never again would anyone look at him and snicker because they recognized his clothes as their old cast-offs!

Two years younger than Menno, he was in Rachel's class in high school. An average student, he never participated in activities outside the required curriculum, and was always alone. He disappeared from Prairie Ridge after completing the requirements for graduation, not waiting for the cap-and-gown ceremony. The principal later delivered his diploma to his mother, who said he had gone to Wichita where he had a job. Through his mother it was learned that, the day after the bombing of Pearl Harbor, he had enlisted in the Air Force.

His anger dissipated, Menno reached over and pulled Rachel close in a comradely hug. "Hey, let's go see a movie!"

The next morning Menno went to church with Rachel and then had dinner at her house. After dinner, wanting to be alone, they went for a drive. With no particular destination in mind, they headed north. When they came to the diagonal cross-country highway, they made a left turn and followed highway 81 through the main street of McPherson. They continued northward until they came to the hill country of the Smoky Hill River. Accustomed to the level farmland in the southern part of the county where the view was restricted by rows of osage orange hedges, they found the hill country fascinating. Leaving the highway, they followed a narrow, dusty road to a sharp incline that led to Coronado Heights, a high butte overlooking the valley of the Smoky Hill River. Legend had it that the Spanish explorer, Francisco Vasquez de Coronado, in his search for the mythical kingdom of Quivira, had, in the sixteenth century, stood on this hill viewing the valley below before returning to the south.

In more recent times, the Civilian Conservation Corps had erected a stone building on the hill's highest point. It was a broad-based tower about twenty feet high, with stone steps inside the fortress-like walls leading to the roof or observation deck.

Menno and Rachel, the only tourists attracted to the sight that afternoon, climbed the stone steps and stared in awe at the broad valley and surrounding hills. The river, flowing from the west, made a wide turn east of their observation point, and went in a northerly direction for many miles before again flowing east. Though the hills on either side of the valley could be used only as grazing land, the floor of the valley was level, and the well ordered farms were proof of the richness of the soil.

Tracing the course of the tree-lined river, they saw it disappear into the hazy atmosphere far in the northeast. Looking out over the hills in all directions, they could see the distant horizon, dimmed by a faint haze. "I guess that's why they're called the Smoky Hills," Menno commented.

They became aware of an offensive odor. Looking for its source, they leaned out over the wide stone wall projecting about three feet above the observation deck. They had been smelling rotting garbage which careless picnickers had strewn around the base of the stone building. Because of the wartime labor shortage, the site was poorly maintained.

Rachel wrinkled her nose. "Let's get out of here," she said.

Pointing to the west, Menno said, "There's a little cedar tree over there. We can sit under it and get out of this hot sun."

Descending the stone steps, they picked their way gingerly around the garbage and beer bottles. They were embarrassed to see, along with the stinking garbage, evidence that the site had been used frequently as a trysting place for lovers.

On the shady side of the little tree which was struggling to grow in the dry, rocky soil, they sat on a big, flat rock, the same color and texture of those used to build the tower.

Rachel sat quietly for several minutes holding Menno's hand. "Well, tomorrow's the day," she said.

"Yeah, but I'll be back by Wednesday. It'll probably be another week or so before I get sent somewhere. I sure hope they send me to Colorado into the forestry service rather than to some mental hospital where I'd be in the bedpan brigade."

Rachel stared at the horizon. "Menno, let's get married."

Menno put both arms around her and held her close for a moment. Then letting her go, he held both her hands in one of his, and with the other behind her head, drew her face to his and kissed her gently. "There is nothing in this whole world I want more than that," he said, "but I think we should wait till we know where I'm going to be. I'm pretty sure it'll be Colorado Springs. If it is, as soon as I get there, I'll have Kate look for a place for us to live. You can come out right away, and we'll find a Mennonite preacher and be married."

"Wouldn't it be nicer to be married in church before you leave? Then, when I join you, we'd already be married."

"I've thought about that, and I think it would be better the other way. In the first place, there wouldn't be enough time to get ready for something like that. A church wedding would mean hundreds of people. We couldn't just invite a few. Everyone else would feel offended. Another thing, I've been thinking, that in wartime, we Mennonites should do as little as possible to attract attention to ourselves. When people see us getting together in big bunches, like at weddings, and having a good time, it makes them hate us all the more for being able to live almost as if there was no war, while their own boys are out there fighting and dying." Silent for a moment, he said, "I'll sure be glad when this stupid war is over, and we can start living again the way we did!"

"There is only one thing I want now," Rachel said, looking at him intently. "No matter what happens, I want to be your wife. I'll go along with whatever plans you make, but I only hope it won't be too long. I need you!"

He pulled her to him again. "I love you, Rachel."

"And I love you, Menno." They sat for a long time clinging to each other.

Later they watched the orange sun go down behind the hazy hills while they munched on the fruit Rachel brought.

9

About nine o'clock the next morning Menno parked his car three blocks from the county court house, where he knew overnight parking was permitted and walked to the courthouse. Joining a group of young men on the north lawn, he recognized some of them, including several relatives.

About ten minutes later the vehicle that was to transport them to Fort Leavenworth pulled up at the curb. It wasn't a regular bus, but a tractor-trailer affair, with the trailer made into a double-decker bus. When the vehicle stopped at the curb, a middle-aged woman, whom Menno recognized as a member of the draft board, moved quickly to stand in front of the door. She held up her hand authoritatively. "You men all stand back on the other side of the sidewalk." The men who had started for the bus moved back. "As I call out your names, you will cross the sidewalk and stand beside the bus."

Reading from a paper on a clipboard, she checked each name as the man stepped forward. Quickly she went through a list of names. "Becker, Blosser, Dirks, Gering." At the name Gering, both Tim and Andy stepped forward. The woman, startled, consulted her clipboard. "Which one of you is Andrew?"

Andy nodded.

"What is your given name?" she demanded, looking at Tim. He told her and she looked at another sheet on her board. "Step back, please."

100

He shrugged and stepped back. She continued her roll call. "Jantz, Kaufman, Koehn, Schrag, Stucky, Toews, Unruh, Zerger." She stopped and said, "I've called you men first because you won't be getting meal vouchers for lunch like the rest of the men." Stepping aside, she motioned them into the bus. Starting the roll call again, she called out the rest of the names alphabetically, and handed each man, including Tim Gering, a meal voucher as he boarded the bus.

As Menno and his group entered the trailer-bus, they saw a steep stairway at the front, leading to the top deck. On the main floor the aisle was on one side instead of the middle, and the seats were wide, padded benches with room for three or four people. About a dozen men sat near the front. The twelve Mennonite men went to the back and sat together. They could hear voices above them, so they knew there were passengers up there, too.

Rachel's nineteen-year-old brother, Paul, shared a bench with Menno. "Boy, she sure separated the sheep from the goats," he said to Menno. "We conshies were very carefully separated and identified. So here we sit, sticking out like sore thumbs."

"We'll just have to take it easy," Menno said. "If anyone starts giving us a hard time, let's just keep our mouths shut. Maybe they'll get tired and leave us alone."

The non-Mennonites began to come in, taking seats directly in front of the Mennonite men. Tim came in with them, and, walking past the others, sat beside Menno on the bench against the back wall. Several years younger, Tim was Menno's cousin. His father and Anna were brother and sister. With his good looks, sense of humor, and ready wit, he had been very popular all through high school, and was usually at the center of any social gathering of his peers. He had little patience with people in authority who took themselves too seriously. One of his favorite pastimes was to study the voice and mannerisms of such people, and entertain his friends by mimicking them. Unpopular teachers in school were favorite targets of ridicule, and he used them to develop his skill as an impressionist.

Today, however, as he sat down beside Menno, his manner suggested that his world was not a happy one. The muscles of his mobile, usually smiling face were contracted into a nervous, pensive expression, as he silently stared straight ahead.

"What was going on out there?" Menno asked. "How come you weren't lumped in with the rest of us oddballs?"

Tim glanced nervously around. "I've got problems."

"Didn't you fill out your form 47?"

"Oh sure, I filled it out, but they turned me down. I'm 1-A."

"Didn't you appeal?"

"Well, dad and I met with the draft board. Dad called in and made an appointment. We got there when they said we should, but had to cool our heels out in the hall for about forty-five minutes. They finally let us into this great big room with a long table at one end, and two straight-backed chairs out in the middle. The guy who opened the door for us motioned us to the two chairs, an' he goes out an' shuts the door."

Warming to his subject, some of the usual animation returned to Tim's mobile features. "I don't know how many there's supposed to be on the draft board, but there were four people sitting in a row behind this long table. When we sat down, they all sat there staring about six inches above our heads. Finally the one on the left says 'Harrumph!' and he shuffles some papers in front of him. Then the one next to him says 'Harrumph!' and shuffles some papers in front of him. The third one was a gray-haired woman with a mustache and shoulders that wide." He measured with his hands. "Well, she says 'Harrumph!' and shuffles her papers. I sit there makin' bets with myself about the fourth one, and sure enough, in about thirty seconds he says 'Harrumph!' and pushes his papers around.

"Nobody says anything for a full minute while the crazy thought keeps goin' through my head that one of them is goin' to slam a wooden mallet down on the table three times and say, 'The prisoner is guilty as charged, and will be taken out and hanged by the neck until dead.' I wanted to bust out laughing, but after a struggle, I convinced myself that this wasn't the time or place for it.

"Finally the guy on the left—I can't think of his name—you know who I mean, he's the ol' guy with the mouse-colored wig. He goes harrumph again, an' I think, if these clowns go through their routine again, I'm gonna crack up for sure. But before the rest of them get a chance to play follow-the-leader again, ol' Mouse-wig looks at Dad an' starts his spiel. 'Mr. Gering, our government has graciously and generously made provision in the selective service law for those who are genuinely opposed, on religious grounds, to participation in war. I don't happen to agree with this provision in the law, thinking it grossly unfair. However, that is beside the point. We are here to administer the selective service law in our county. Since there are a large number of you people in our county, we have great difficulty each month filling our quota of military draftees. One of our duties as members of this board is to make judgments as to the sincerity of those applying for exemption from military conscription.'

"All the time he's talking, his upper teeth keep falling down, making a loud click when they hit his lowers. Well, when this happens, usually right in the middle of a word, he clamps his jaws together real tight, trying to make his uppers stick up there where they belong. Well, it's no use. Another six-and-a-half words, and, CLICK! down they come again. Of course all this time he's trying to look real authoritative and fierce. Only he has eyes exactly like a sad old Basset hound, and can you imagine how fierce and authoritative you can look if you have eyes like a basset hound, and your teeth keep falling down?

"Well, the ol' guy reached up and scratched the back of his head, and his wig slid forward about an inch. Having a lower forehead didn't seem to bother him any, and he goes on. 'We have reason to believe your son does not qualify as a religious pacifist. In the past several years he has become well known to our county sheriff's department, and to our local police. He

103

drives his car in a manner that makes of it a lethal weapon. Hardly an act of a pacifist!'

"When he said this he raised his John L. Lewis eyebrows, making deep wrinkles in his forehead. I can't figure out how anybody could have John L. Lewis eyebrows on top of basset hound eyes, but this ol' guy has 'em! Well, anyway, when he brings those eyebrows down again, the ridges between the wrinkles drag the wig down to where it was touching his eyebrows. You can imagine the fix I was in. The ol' guy was so funny he was crackin' me up, but I just couldn't bust out laughing at the judge who was listing my crimes an' was about to pass sentence. With no forehead left now at all, the ol' guy goes on, his mousy wig moving up an' down, riding on his eyebrows. 'On several occasions in the past year, your son has been discovered by members of the sheriff's department in an inebriated condition, in the company of his ruffian friends, at illegal roadside beer-drinking parties. It is the unanimous finding of this board that your son, Timothy James Gering, does not qualify for military exemption on religious grounds. That is all. Good day.'

"So here I am—on my way to fight for God and country!" Thinking a moment, he said, "You know, the ol' guy was right. I have been raisin' all kinds o' hell, but man, there's no way I can take a gun an' go out an' kill people! If I can get out of this mess, I'm gonna straighten up an' fly right. If I can get a 4-F or something, I'll hightail it back to the farm, an', till this war is over, you won't see me anywhere but on the farm and in church."

"How could you manage a 4-F? You look pretty healthy to me," Menno said.

Tim seemed to be thinking for a moment, then, leaning toward Menno, said, in a low, conspiratorial tone, "I've got a plan that I'm pretty sure will get me out of this."

"Don't do anything that'll get you in trouble."

"Trouble!? I'm in trouble now. It couldn't get any worse! Hey," he smiled, relaxed, "if my plan works, I'll tell you all about it, but remember, it's just between the two of us. Okay?"

Engrossed in their own conversation, they hadn't noticed that several seats ahead of them the talking was becoming loud and heated. The three men in the seat immediately behind the men going into the army were members of the Holdeman Mennonite church. All three remained silent as the men in the seat ahead of them began taunting them, ridiculing their beards which their church required they wear. The Mennonite men in the seat behind the Holdeman men, however, rose to the bait, and began to argue with the young draftees who claimed to be offended by the Mennonite doctrine of nonresistance. The main spokesman for the pro-military was a beefy, florid faced young man of about twenty. He became more and more excited as he raved and ranted against the "cowardly" conscientious objectors. Most of his raving was directed at Harry Toews, who kept returning his insults. Harry, like Tim, was also well known to law enforcement officers, but because he lived in the extreme southern part of the county and ran around with his rowdy friends in Harvey county, his own draft board didn't know him, and had approved his application for conscientious objector status. Largely ignorant of the basis for the Mennonite doctrine of nonresistance, Harry made a number of contradictory and foolish statements that only served to further anger his antagonists.

"Why doesn't he shut up?" Menno groaned. "He's making us all look like a bunch of jerks."

Physical violence was averted when a heavy, big-boned, middle-aged man, dressed in a Santa Fe bus driver's uniform, came down the stairs from the upper deck. He put his hand on the shoulder of the florid-faced young man, who, by then, was standing in the aisle facing his opponent and telling him how he was going to radically rearrange his facial features. Feeling the hand on his shoulder, he whirled around.

"Hey, take it easy kid. I'm on your side," the older man said with a grin. "I think you oughta wait, though, 'til you get a uniform on, an' get over there before you start doin' in Krauts. In

105

the meantime you better go up them stairs an' find a seat up there. The atmosphere's better up there, anyhow." He stood in the aisle and watched the young man disappear up the steps before sitting in the seat he had vacated.

The trailer-bus stopped at the courthouse in Marion, picking up more men, and again at Emporia. On the outskirts of Ottawa, the driver pulled in to a truck stop for a lunch break. The man in the bus driver's uniform, acting as a conductor, told everyone they would be there for an hour. The restaurant, which catered mostly to truck drivers, was well back from the road, giving the truckers plenty of room to park their rigs while they ate.

The big, flat-roofed building was filled with booths, tables, and counter stools. The place was already more than half filled with truckers, so the men from the trailer-bus sat wherever they could find space.

When the hour was almost up, the trailer-bus began to reload as the men straggled out of the restaurant. The Mennonite men were the first in, and took their same seats. The man in the bus-driver uniform stood beside the door as the men returned to the bus. When the beefy young troublemaker got on, he hesitated at the bottom of the stairs, and, making sure all the Mennonite men saw him, he gave them a contemptuous smirk before going up the steep stairs.

When the conductor thought all the men were back, he came in, and halfway up the stairs, bellowed at the men in the upper deck, "Everybody here?" Apparently they were. He backed down the stairs and was about to yell the same question to the lower deck, when Conrad Becker, the oldest of the three bearded men, stood in the aisle and said, "We're missing a man."

"Well, go find him!"

Conrad signaled Art Koehn to follow him, and the two men ran to the restaurant. It was only then that the rest of the Mennonites realized that Danny Unruh hadn't come back to the bus.

The conductor paced back and forth beside the bus. In about ten minutes the three men returned. Becker and Koehn were supporting Danny Unruh between them. He walked with his head down, and stumbled several times. Everyone stared at the trio as they came through the door and made their way to their seat. Danny, small and fine-boned, looking sixteen rather than nineteen, was missing his whispy, blond beard. In its place were ugly cuts on his chin and along his jaws. Blood had run down from the cuts and coagulated. Keeping his face turned toward the floor, he hoped no one would see that he had been crying.

The conductor signaled the driver to start. He took his seat, pretending not to notice the men on the bench behind him. The lower floor was quiet as the trailer-bus traveled downtown to the Franklin County courthouse.

Danny, sitting between Conrad and Art, hunched forward, his arms pressed against his stomach. Conrad laid his hand on his narrow shoulders, awkwardly trying to comfort him.

The passengers boarding at the courthouse climbed the steps to the upper deck. Continuing through town, the driver soon had them on the northbound highway toward Lawrence. Out on the open road, normal conversation on the lower deck resumed. The Mennonites could talk among themselves again without fear of being overheard. Harry Toews, chastened and very quiet after coming close to having his pacifism put to the test, leaned forward and asked Conrad Becker, "What happened back there?"

Twisting around so that he faced directly backward and would not be heard by the non-Mennonites nearest him, he said, "They caught him in the washroom and threw him through the window. One of 'em was waitin' outside and held him 'til the others got there. There were three of 'em. You can see what they did to him."

"Was one of 'em the big-mouth that was down here and got sent upstairs?" Harry asked.

Conrad nodded. He had had to speak in a low voice, so what

he said was repeated farther back for the benefit of those on the back bench.

An anger that would not go away was beginning to build up in Menno.

Another stop in Lawrence at the Douglas County courthouse filled the trailer-bus completely. The next stop was at the Fort Leavenworth induction center where men in uniform met them, checked their papers, and directed them to various barracks. They were told where the mess hall was located, when meals would be served, and where they were to report for physicals at nine the next morning. The conscientious objectors were housed in separate barracks where Menno and his companions met other Mennonites as well as Quakers and members of other peace churches.

The next morning, after a mess-hall breakfast, a crowd of recruits began gathering at the side of the building in which they were to get their physicals. By the time someone opened the door at nine o'clock, the crowd had grown to several hundred. When they got inside they found themselves in a huge locker room. At the far end of the room a stairway led to a door about midway between the floor and the ceiling of the locker room. A man in uniform stood on the top step in front of the closed door. He began yelling to the draftees below him. "All right men, get your clothes off, an' I mean all of 'em. Find a locker an' put 'em in. There's a chain with a key on it hangin' on a hook inside. Put your clothes an' valuables in the locker, lock 'em up, hang the chain around your neck, an' then line up along this wall over here by these steps." He repeated this over and over as more and more men came through the outside door. The room became so crowded that the men, pressed together shoulder to shoulder, had difficulty removing their clothes.

A line began to form against the wall and up the steps. Several men had left their shorts on. The uniformed man pointed at them and bellowed, "You there! Get undressed. All of it!" He finally opened the door, and the naked men began to file through into a room the size of a football field. A number of desks were scattered at random over the huge floor. Uniformed officers sat behind each desk. Most desks had some sort of medical paraphernalia on or beside them, indicating the men behind them were military doctors. Other men in uniform walked around the room shouting at the draftees, separating them into groups and directing them to various desks.

Menno had been to the stockyards in Wichita several times when Jonas had shipped cattle or hogs. He had felt deep compassion for the confused and frightened animals and anger toward the men, who, unfeelingly, whipped and goaded the helpless animals from pen to pen.

He began to think of himself as part of a great herd of naked, vulnerable animals, goaded and pushed from place to place. He noticed that no one ever looked directly into the eyes of anyone else; the naked men, feeling degraded and exposed, didn't want to reveal their feelings to one another. The uniformed men, wearing their uniforms like armor, didn't look directly at the naked draftees because they saw them, not as fellow human beings, but as objects to be moved about on command.

Menno's smoldering anger grew at a world gone awry.

Lines of about a half-dozen men were constantly forming at each desk. Each doctor examined a different part of the anatomy. There were uniformed assistants at each desk who shouted orders at the men. At one desk a man kept shouting, "All right, skin it back, an' milk it down!" and each, in turn, was examined for discharge which might indicate veneral disease. At another desk an assistant kept shouting, "Bend over, spread your cheeks and cough!" After each examination the examining doctor recorded the results on papers on his desk and put his initials in the appropriate place on the papers carried by the draftees.

At noon several long tables on wheels were brought into the room, each loaded with milk, coffee, and sandwiches. The men, between examinations, helped themselves.

Menno, occupied with his own angry thoughts, was unaware that Tim, who had been near him since entering the building, had become nervous and pensive. About two o'clock, Menno and Tim, along with several others, were ordered to another desk. By the equipment on it they knew their blood pressure was to be taken. The assistant lined them up in a row in front of the desk and shouted, "All right now, jump up and down on your left foot!" The doctor behind the desk continued to make check marks on a form before him, not looking up. Suddenly Menno was aware that Tim, at the opposite end of the line, had stopped jumping and was leaning over the desk, staring at the doctor. Looking up to see Tim's face not two feet from his own, the doctor involuntarily jerked back. "What the hell? Get back in line and keep jumping!"

Tim didn't move, but continued to stare like a wild-eyed zealot at the doctor, who by now, was looking around for his assistant. The assistant had turned his back for a moment to talk to another uniform. The doctor opened his mouth to speak again, but Tim, staring deeply into his eyes, asked, "Wouldn't you like to be saved?"

"Look son, get—" He pointed to the spot on which Tim was supposed to be jumping.

Before the command could be completed, Tim moved even closer, his eyes aflame with holy zeal. "Please," his zeal combined with deep compassion, "won't you receive Jesus into your heart and escape the terrible judgment of Almighty God?"

The doctor opened a drawer and took out a scratch pad. Looking exhausted, he said to no one in particular, "Oh God, what a day!" On the scratch pad he wrote in large letters, "This man for Dr. Ginsberg." Tearing off the top sheet, he handed it to Tim. "Son," he said, pointing to the far corner of the large room, "you see that door over there in the corner?"

Tim nodded.

"Well, through that door you'll see a long hallway. All along that hallway are doors with names on them. When you come to the door with this name on it, you go in and give this to the man sitting at the desk."

A puzzled frown on his face, Tim took the note. He was about to say something, but was silenced with, "Just go! Okay?"

Passing behind the doctor on the way to the designated doorway, he resisted the temptation to turn and wink at Menno.

Jumping up and down on one foot, Menno thought, "Of course! I should have guessed what that crazy kid was up to." Menno remembered the times Tim had told him about his mother's brother who had moved to Wichita and joined a church known for its evangelistic fervor. Whenever he visited Tim's family he kept trying to convert them. Tim, a born actor, remembered all the strange things he said so that he could repeat them later, while mimicking his uncle's peculiar mannerisms and nasal voice. Now he had maneuvered himself into a chance to see an army psychiatrist, where, with his acting ability and his knowledge of evangelistic jargon, he could convince the army he was mentally and emotionally unfit for service. "This was what he meant when he mentioned a 4-F on the bus. Why didn't I stop him?" Menno reproved himself. "He's just a farm kid, and he's up against professionals! They'll see right through him. Instead of a 4-F, they'll give him five years in the federal pen right here in Leavenworth."

10

Tim, carrying the various forms he had been accumulating all day plus the note, walked down the hall and found the door marked DR. GINSBERG. The door was partly open, and he could see the uniformed psychiatrist, alone in the room, working at his desk.

Tim approached the desk slowly, holding the note in front of him. Finished with the paper he was working on, the doctor looked up. Without saying anything, he took the paper, glanced at it, and laid it on his desk. "Hand me the papers you're holding, please."

Tim handed them to him.

"Sit down," he pointed to a straight-backed chair about six feet in front of the desk. As he looked over the papers, he said, "Who gave you this note?"

"A doctor out there," Tim pointed vaguely in the direction of the large, central room.

"You must have talked to him. What did you say?"

"Well, the man looked so sad, I knew he didn't have the Lord Jesus in his heart, so I asked him if he wanted to be saved."

"How did he react to your question?"

"Well, he didn't really answer me, but I could tell he was very troubled, so I asked him if he didn't want to take Jesus as his Lord and Savior and escape the terrible judgment of God, because I believe that was what he was really troubled about.

112

That's why he looked so sad."

"What did he say then?"

"Well, he didn't really say anything. He just wrote that note and told me to come here. I was sorry to have to leave him, because I think I could have shown him the way. But I'm praying that the Holy Spirit will continue to convict him of sin, and bring him to a saving knowledge of the Lord Jesus Christ."

The psychiatrist kept taking sheets of unlined paper from a stack beside him, writing down everything that was said. He was a fast writer, and wrote so large that there were never more than three or four words on a line, and no more than six or seven lines on a page. "Tell me," Dr. Ginsberg said, "do you ever have visions?"

"The vision that changed my life forever was that of the Lord Jesus Christ hanging on Calvary's cross, bleeding and dying for me. I fell on my face before the awful majesty of God-made-flesh, and dying that I might have life, and have it eternally. I cried out, 'God be merciful to me, a sinner, and save me for Jesus' sake!' "

Pretending he was recalling the experience, Tim tilted his head back, half closed his eyes, and smiled as though he was being sung to by a chorus of angels. He was, of course, mimicking his uncle, except that he didn't employ the nasal tone. "God reached down with tender, loving care and lifted me up from the miry clay and set my feet upon a rock. He established my way. He put a new song in my heart. I was born again, and his Spirit witnessed with my spirit that I was his child. Such ecstasy and glory cannot be contained. I am constrained to show others the way!"

Writing frantically to keep up, the doctor glanced toward the open door. Whenever, out of the corner of his eye, he saw other officers passing, he motioned them in. The sheets of paper with the record of the conversation were passed around to the officers as the room began to fill up.

Tim became increasingly aware that what he was doing was dishonest as well as a betrayal of his own religious convictions.

He was taking the name of the Lord in vain. At the same time, he realized he didn't have the moral courage to stop it and confess his wrongdoing to his interrogator. He knew that such a confession would bring swift reprisal. He had to brazen his way through. Would he hear a rooster crow when it was over?

While this was going through his mind, he missed a question put to him by Dr. Ginsberg, but since he had maintained, out of fear of discovery, a facial expression of blissful repose, the doctor supposed he was listening either to the voice of God or a chorus of angels, and patiently asked the question again. "Have you had any other visions?"

"Oh yes," Tim said, "just a few weeks ago I was reading from the Word where Jesus said, 'The fields are white unto the harvest, but the labourers are few. Go ye therefore into all nations, making disciples from among all men.' Well, I sat back and got a vision of thousands, even millions of men marching into battle, and there were dark shadows over many of them. I knew they were going to die in battle, and the words came to me, 'Go, for the labourers are few.' And the next day I got my notice from the president, and I knew it was the voice of God telling me what I must do."

"What was it the voice of God told you to do?"

"Why, to join the army and bring the good news of the gospel of the saving grace of Jesus to all those lost men who are going to die in battle."

By this time there were several dozen sheets of paper being passed around among the room full of army officers. The older ones, the fatherly looking ones, read and then looked at Tim with compassion and pity. The younger ones read and stared at him in openmouthed incredulity.

"You have then been in communication with God, and he has somehow told you to join the army so you can save souls?"

"Oh, I can't save souls! Only God can do that."

"I don't understand. If that is the case, what is your function in all this?"

"The apostle Peter said, 'Be ready to give to every man the

114

reason for the hope that lieth within you.' So my function—my commission—is to witness to others of the saving power of Jesus, to lead them to the fountain of amazing grace, to invite them to come to the foot of the cross to confess their sins and be born again into the kingdom of God, and to know the blessed joy of eternal salvation."

While Tim sat in a smiling trance, seeming to be contemplating his part in the Great Commission, the psychiatrist finished writing. Leaning back in his chair, with elbows on the armrests, he twirled his pencil with both hands. He exchanged glances and shakes of the head with an older man in a well-decorated uniform with stars on his shoulders, then turned again to Tim. "Would you mind stepping out into the hall? I would like to confer for a moment with General Adams."

Still smiling, Tim stepped into the hall. The general made a gesture, dismissing all the lesser officers. One by one they went out the door, each staring at Tim as he stepped past him, giving him a wide berth. Tim smiled and nodded to each one. Out of the corner of his eye he could see that, about thirty feet down the hall, as if on cue, each one turned to give him another look. The last officer to leave the room pulled the door shut behind him, stared at Tim, and slipped quickly by him. Tim smiled and nodded. Thirty feet down the hall the man turned for another look. "Oh well," Tim said to himself, "they'll have something to talk about in the officers' quarters tonight."

A moment later the door opened and the general motioned him in. The doctor said, "I have only another question or two, and then you can go."

Tim looked at him, smiling in anticipation.

Ginsberg fiddled with his pencil. "What would you say if, in spite of your eagerness to join the armed forces, the army had decided not to accept you?"

Determined to act out the charade to the end, Tim sat down hard on the chair. His face, at first, registered total disbelief, then bewilderment, as if he was saying to himself, "But I was so sure I heard the voice of God!"

The two officers watched patiently as Tim's expressive face revealed the progression of his spiritual struggle, moving from the agony of dashed hopes, to questioning his own spirituality, to a final, peaceful resignation and acceptance of the right of a sovereign God to thus put his faith to the test. The doctor's question was answered when Tim bowed his head, and quietly but fervently said, "Father, not my will, but thine be done."

Reaching into a drawer the doctor pulled out an ink pad and a large rubber stamp. Inking the stamp, he carefully transmitted REJECTED on the bottom line of one of Tim's papers.

Leaning over the desk, the general gave the paper a half turn, and added his signature. Handing the paper to Tim, he patted him on the shoulder, saying, "I'm sorry, son." Tim could hear real compassion in his voice.

One of the last to be finished with his physical examination, Menno was finally free to go to the locker room and put on his clothes. Before leaving the big room he cast another anxious glance toward the door through which Tim had disappeared. After he had dressed he decided to go back to the big room and wait for him. He paced back and forth near the locker-room door, glancing every few minutes at the clock on the wall. At three-thirty, he finally decided that Tim wasn't coming back. He was sure he was being held in a cell somewhere nearby, while some prosecutor was writing up charges of attempted draft evasion.

He left the building and started walking slowly and aimlessly toward the barracks. He was angry at himself for not having guessed ahead of time what Tim was up to, and stopped him from attempting something so foolhardy. He was angry at the whole gone-crazy world, and, even though he hadn't quite formed it into conscious thought, he was angry at God, whom he could no longer depend on because he was letting all this happen. His anger and frustration grew as he reviewed the events of the past two days.

Hearing laughter, he looked to his left and saw a clump of

116

bushes. He started to look away when he saw, rising above the bushes, a pair of bare feet being pulled up by two pairs of hands grasping the ankles. Curious, he walked around the bushes. Young Danny Unruh, his clothes torn off, was being held upside down by two tall young men. The beefy, florid faced bully who had attacked him in Ottawa had a small can of yellow paint and a two-inch brush, and was painting a stripe from Danny's buttocks to his neck.

Bellowing with rage, Menno leaped. The young man whirled, the can in one hand and the brush in the other. His reflexes were too slow to allow him to assume a defensive position and he took Menno's powerful fist in his paunchy stomach. The two men holding Danny threw him into the bushes and fled. The can and brush dropped to the ground as the recruit's knees buckled and he slumped forward. Grabbing his hair with his left hand and jerking the bully's head back, Menno, with all the power he could put into it, smashed his right fist into the face before him. That face embodied all the dark evil he had witnessed since leaving home. Holding on to the mop of hair, he smashed his fist again and again into the face. Finally, the hair, slippery with hair-oil, slipped from his grasp and the man fell backward onto the grass. Menno, his chest heaving, stood with his feet almost touching those of the now unconscious man.

Leaning forward, he put his hands on his knees and stared at the face he had just smashed. The florid complexion had become the color of bleached-flour bread dough. Bright red blood bubbled and trickled from between the torn lips, and slowly oozed from the flattened, swelling nose. Lying on the ground, the man looked small—like a battered child. Menno stared. Drained now of his anger, a look of horror took control of his features. He sank to his knees, clutching his head in his hands. The evil monster that had been chained in the dark recesses of his heart had broken loose and carried him over the precipice into the dark void, infinite and terrible, that had been waiting to receive him.

He turned and retched. Again and again he retched. He was only dimly aware of what was happening when two military policemen grabbed him from behind, handcuffing his wrists together behind his back. They pulled him along between them, walking briskly down the broad concrete walk.

Danny moaned and crawled out of the bushes.

As Tim came through the door he glanced at the wall clock. It was three-thirty-two. Exhausted from nervous tension, he made his way to the locker room. It was empty. He retrieved his clothes from the locker and sat down on a wooden bench. He began to tremble. He covered his face with his hands, and began to shake with sobs. "Oh God! What have I done?" In a few moments he regained control and began putting on his clothes. He would go back to the psychiatrist and tell him it was all a lie.

He knocked on Ginsberg's door several times. There was no response. He turned the knob. The door was locked. He was about to ask someone where he could find the psychiatrist, when he realized again he didn't have the courage to face the consequences. What was done was done. He'd have to live with it.

Outside the building he decided to go to the barracks to see if he could find Menno. Halfway there, he saw two MPs emerge from behind a clump of bushes with a man in civilian clothes between them. The man's hands were manacled behind him. His head was slumped forward, his chin on his chest. When they reached the sidewalk, they turned and walked in the same direction Tim was going. He could see only their backs, but he had an uneasy feeling that the man in the middle was someone he should know.

About to quicken his pace so that he could get closer, he heard noises on his left. Just past the bushes, he recognized Danny Unruh sitting on the grass, naked and sobbing. Looking again at the MPs and their prisoner, he gasped, "Oh God, no! It's Menno!"

118

He almost started to run after them when he realized there was nothing he could do. Turning to the scene behind the bushes, he recognized the man on the ground and realized what had happened. Several men in uniform were standing around or squatting beside the unconscious man.

Danny was sitting with his arms around his knees, resting his forehead on them. Tim gathered up his torn clothing from where it was strewn in the grass and hanging from the bushes. Talking quietly to him, comforting him as one would comfort an injured child, Tim helped him dress. He could hear a screaming ambulance approaching.

One of the MPs unlocked Menno's handcuffs while the other opened the cell door. Pushing him into the six-by-eight-foot cell, he said, "There ya go, tiger."

Locking the door, the other joked, "Man, with a killer like that on our side, them Krauts an' Japs ain't got a chance!"

Both chuckled as they walked away.

There was a toilet without a seat in one corner of the cell, with a small lavatory sink beside it. Along one wall was a steel slab covered with a thin mattress. A low-watt bulb in a ceiling fixture outside the cell cast a dim light.

Menno sat on the mattress, elbows on his knees, his hands extended before him. He stared at them. They seemed to him to be red, covered with blood. He had shed the blood of a fellow man. Maybe killed him. Blood had come out of the man's mouth, his nose.

There is a fountain filled with blood.

He covered his face with his hands.

What hast thou done? the voice of thy brother's blood crieth unto me from the ground.

Please God, don't let the man die!
Is your concern for the man you bludgeoned, or for yourself?

—his blood will I require at thine hand.

Murderer!

and murderers . . . shall have their part in the lake which burneth with fire and brimstone.

No!

Who is this man with the mark of Cain?

My religious conviction forbids me to participate in war. I am a Mennonite. We are a people of peace. We live by the rules of the-kingdom-that-is-not-of-this-world. The law we obey is the law of love. We abhor violence and war.

Bulletin!

Conscientious Objector Murders Fellow Draftee.

Mennonite man, claiming exemption from military duty on the grounds his religion forbids him to engage in war or violence, brutally attacks fellow draftee at induction center. With bare fists, beats him to death.

Menno lay on his back on the mattress, his hands clasped behind his head, his unseeing eyes fixed on the ceiling. Unaware of the passage of time, he finally drifted into sleep. He dreamed that Rachel appeared at the bars. He held out his hands to her. She saw the blood dripping from them and turned away, loathing and disgust on her face. Jonas and Anna stood looking at him, sadly shaking their heads before turning away.

Someone was yelling at him. Slowly turning his head, he saw two MPs through the bars. One was shouting, "I ain't gonna tell ya again, Killer. I said, on your feet! An' I mean now!"

While Menno was slowly moving his stiffened limbs, preparing to stand up, the other, seeing a plate of food under the bars, said in a Southern drawl, "Why looka here, he ain't even touched his breakfast."

Menno stood beside the steel slab and mattress, his dull face and clouded eyes turned toward the uniformed men.

"Got the cuffs?" one asked.

"Aw, I don't think we need 'em. He looks pretty tame this morning'," the other one said.

The Southerner unlocked the cell door and drawled, "Aw-right, Killer, you-all come out'n there now an' start walkin' 'tween us, but if'n you-all try anythin' funny, the two of us is gonna be all over you like mud on a wallowin' hog! You-all get my meanin'?"

Moving like an automaton, Menno was marched down a long corridor, up several sets of stairs, and down another corridor. Halfway down, they turned left through an open door. Only vaguely aware of his surroundings, he was escorted to a long bench along one wall. He sat between the two MPs. A young woman in a WAC uniform sat behind a desk in a corner of the twenty-foot square room. She picked up the telephone on the desk and spoke briefly into it, then continued working at her typewriter.

From where the men sat on the bench they could see a huge, fortress-like building with a great aluminum colored dome about a mile away to the southwest.

"Hey, Killer," one of the MPs said, "see that great big building 'way over there? That's the federal pen. Wanna take a look at your new home?"

The telephone rang above the clatter of the typewriter. The WAC picked it up, listened a moment, said, "Yes, sir," and then replaced it. Looking at the men and pointing her thumb over her shoulder to the door behind her, she said, "He's ready now."

After going through the door, the MPs fell in beside Menno, and, each holding an arm, marched him to a position in front of a large desk at the far end of the room. Releasing his arms, they took two steps backward and stood at attention.

The bald man in the padded, leather-covered armchair behind the desk was absorbed in reading papers in an open file-folder. Judging by the amount of metal decorating his uniform,

121

he was a high-ranking officer. Ignoring the men standing in front of his desk, he continued to read. Finally finished, he looked up. He stared at Menno, without expression, for a full thirty seconds. "You're Menno Schrag." It was a statement, not a question.

Menno nodded.

"Well, Menno Schrag, I've just been through some very interesting reading material. Very interesting indeed." He continued to stare at Menno, a bemused expression on his face.

Adjusting his position as if indicating he was now ready to get down to business, he said, "I should preface my remarks by saying that since neither you nor your victim are members of the military, this is a problem for the civilian authorities and not a military one. However, since the incident in question occurred on a military post, it is our duty to make a preliminary investigation before turning you over to the civilian authorities.

"In spite of the uncommon viciousness of your brutal attack, the hospital report this morning indicates your victim will live. X rays show bone fragments from the shattered face were very close to penetrating the brain. One more blow would certainly have resulted in death.

"Assault cases on a military base this large are not uncommon. However, when the officer reported this one to me, he mentioned the story had a rather unique twist. He told me your classification was IV-E. I must confess my interest was piqued. I sent for your file, and, in the light of your activities yesterday afternoon, it makes very interesting reading."

Looking through the file before him, the man went on. "It appears that, until recently, you have been deferred as a farmer. For reasons not stated in your file, you became ineligible for the deferment, and were classified 1-A. You immediately filled out form 47, asking for exemption from military duty on grounds of conscientious objection to war. In addition to answering all the questions on the form, you included a well-written letter to your draft board, elaborating on your deep-felt religious pacifism. In your letter you describe yourself as a disciple of the prince of peace, who tells his followers to love their enemies, do good to those who spitefully use you, and so on, and so on, and that for conscience' sake, you cannot participate in war.

"All in all, the appeal for conscientious objector status was well written, and the writer appears very sincere. I can see that your draft board would, under the existing draft law, be inclined to grant your request. Reading the papers in your file, I see you as a pacifist, Mennonite, conscientious objector. Then I read this." He held up a typewritten paper. "This is a report of a man who, with his bare fists, bludgeoned another man to the point of death! Which of these men are you?" He looked at Menno, his manner and tone demanding an answer.

All the time the man was speaking, Menno was only dimly aware of what he was saying. He was floating somewhere in a dark, bottomless pit. The face before him floated in gray fog. It seemed to recede and advance as it threatened and accused him. Suddenly he realized that he had been asked a question and he was required to give an answer. He had the feeling the question was the most important one ever put to him. As the man's eyes bored into him, Menno struggled to put the pieces together. "Which one of these men are you?" The question seemed to be about good and evil, about light and darkness. But hadn't he already answered the question? He had renounced everything that was good and holy, and had embraced evil and darkness. When he opened his mouth to speak, it was so dry that only an unintelligible sound came out.

"What did you say? Speak up!"

Struggling to bring moisture into his mouth while the officer continued to stare demandingly at him, Menno finally said, slowly, but distinctly, "I want to join the army."

11

The officer took a deep breath, leaned back in his chair, and exhaled loudly. He continued to stare at Menno, a smile playing at the corners of his mouth. He was about to indulge himself with a cat-and-mouse game with this Mennonite farmer who claimed to be a pacifist and then tried to kill a man. Thinking again of Menno's statement that he wanted to join the army, he asked himself, "Why not?" A speculative look replaced his bemused smile. It would be a waste of manpower to turn him over to the civilian authorities who would put him in jail somewhere. His attack, after all, was not unprovoked. He certainly demonstrated his willingness to fight for his friends. Men on the front don't, after all, fight for such abstract things as God and country. When push comes to shove, they fight to keep themselves and their friends from getting killed. Three months of basic training will completely erase all this pacifism nonsense from his mind. Especially so, since he has already appeared to have made up his mind it's not for him.

While these thoughts were going through his mind, he stared speculatively at Menno. "Very well, Menno Schrag, we'll see what we can do."

Addressing the MPs who had been standing at attention all this time, he said, "Take this man back to the outer office and wait there with him until I want him again."

As the military policemen escorted Menno from the room, the officer picked up his phone. He knew how to cut through red tape and go around idiotic bureaucrats.

About twenty minutes later the phone on the outer office desk buzzed. Speaking into it for a few seconds, the WAC replaced the phone and again motioned with her thumb, indicating the men were wanted inside.

Assuming their previous positions, the three men faced the desk. Shuffling papers as though he was already engrossed in other, more important matters, the officer, scarcely looking up, said, "There will be an induction ceremony at fifteen hundred hours today in the usual place. You will remain in the custody of these military police officers until then. They will escort you to the place of induction. Dismissed!"

At three that afternoon, Menno found himself on the end of a long line of recruits facing an officer reading from a book. After being told to take one step forward, the recruits were informed they were now members of the United States Army.

The bus on which Menno, Tim, and the others had come to Fort Leavenworth left about an hour after Menno had been taken into custody. The young draftees were tired after a hard day. Many slept until they were left off at their various court houses. It was well after midnight when Tim was at last able to get off and walk to his car. It was parked beside Menno's. He drove home, carefully observing the speed limit.

At nine the next morning, he drove to the Tobias Kaufman farm and told Rachel all he knew about what had happened. She was already concerned that something had gone wrong. During breakfast, her brother Paul was noncommittal when pressed for details of his experiences at Fort Leavenworth. He wouldn't look directly at Rachel and hurried out of the house immediately after eating.

The younger children were in school when Tim arrived, and Paul and his father were out planting wheat.

When Tim said he was going to tell Jonas and Anna, Rachel asked to go with him. When they arrived at the Schrag farm Anna was alone in the house, and Jonas was planting wheat in the field west of the barn. Anna ran to the field as he approached the end nearest the house. In a few minutes he came with her to the house. No one seemed to know what to do, or how to get more information. Finally Jonas said, "If we don't hear anything by early tomorrow morning, we'll drive to Fort Leavenworth."

The next morning, Jonas, Anna, and Rachel made the trip, arriving in midafternoon. At the post office in the town of Leavenworth they were told the fort was just north of town. At the main gate a guard directed them to the administration building.

Each time they told their story, they were directed to another office. After talking to secretaries wearing WAC uniforms in four offices, one finally said, "Well, if what you say is true, his file wouldn't be here, but I'll check anyway." Opening a file drawer, she ran her fingers over the file tabs. Suddenly she stopped, and, turning around, asked, "Did you say your son's name is Menno Schrag?"

"Yes."

"According to his file, yesterday at fifteen hundred hours, he voluntarily enlisted, and was inducted into the army." Noting something unusual about the file, she quickly read through it. She was, coincidentally, a Quaker who had made a decision against pacifism and joined the Women's Army Corps. Having made the decision after much soul-searching, she was moved and sympathetic when she saw the shock and disbelief on the faces before her. "I'm sorry," she said. "Is there anything I can do to help?"

"May we see him?" Rachel asked, her eyes brimming.

"I'm sorry. He's been sent to another base and is in basic training. Basic training lasts for three months, and the men are not allowed visitors during this time. When it is over they are given short furloughs before being issued orders."

"Are they allowed letters?"

"Oh yes. Here, I'll give you the address where you can write to him." Consulting the file, she wrote the appropriate code letters and numbers, along with "Fort Leonard Wood, Missouri," on a paper and handed it to Rachel.

It was past midnight when Rachel was delivered to her home, and Jonas and Anna drove to theirs.

The first few days of basic training were a continuation of Menno's nightmare. In spite of his despair, however, he had the urge to survive. Somehow he knew that to do so, he must discover some kind of meaning to the never-ending movements around him and to the continuous cacophony of sound that threatened to overwhelm him. Taking his cue from the movements of the other recruits, he began to figure out a certain order he was expected to follow. The bellowing and screaming of the sergeants was harder to figure out. For the most part, Menno ignored it. He did not understand that a very important part of the training sergeant's job is to emit a steady stream of obscene insults to the new recruits until any feeling of self-worth they possess is completely obliterated. Once this is accomplished, the trainer's job is then to restore slowly to the trainees confidence in themselves, not as individual human beings with individual self-worth, but as components of an efficient fighting unit. This is called making soldiers out of boys.

This psychological manipulation was lost on Menno, whose experience the day before his induction had already, in his own mind, stripped him of his humanity. The haranguing insults of the sergeants, designed to debase him, came across to him as merely noise. He already saw himself as debased and without value.

The daily exercises, pushing the recruits to the limits of their physical endurance, made sleep at night come easy. It also made it easier for Menno to turn off his thinking as he pushed his body to its absolute limits. Without realizing it, he was engaging in self-flagellation.

One evening, about a week after arriving at the training center, while Menno prepared for his bunk and oblivion, he heard his name called. Looking in the direction of the sound, he saw a soldier with a handful of letters standing on a table calling out names. Menno walked slowly toward the table. All the letters in the man's hand were now gone except one. Looking at it, he called out Menno's name again. Menno reached for it and saw Rachel's name in the upper left-hand corner. Slowly he walked back to his bunk, not taking his eyes from Rachel's name. He sat on his bunk several minutes before finally opening the letter. It was a long letter in which she poured out her love for him. She wrote that she thought she understood what had happened, and assured him that things were going to be all right again. She pleaded with him to write to her, to share this terrible experience with her, and not to try to bear it all alone. Love casts out fear and evil, and the love of God and their love for each other would overcome the evil that was threatening to destroy them both. If he could forgive himself, surely God, in his love, would forgive him.

Slowly Menno put the letter back in its envelope. His hands trembled. Tears sprang to his eyes. His love for her was an excruciating ache, but how could she still love him? He who was guilty of such monstrous, loathsome evil. Love casts out evil, she wrote.

"Dear Rachel," he wrote on the tablet. He gripped the pencil. How could he put into words for her what he didn't understand himself? How could he tell her about the pit he had fallen into? The void? He put the writing tablet and pencil under his pillow and stretched himself out on his cot.

The lights went out and the men around him settled into sleep. Menno stared into the dark. "There is only thing I want now," Rachel had said on Coronado Heights, "no matter what happens, I want to be your wife." He knew she had forgiven him the suffering he had caused her.

Would the man against whom he had so grievously sinned forgive him?

He covered his face with his hands. Would God forgive him?

If we confess our sins, he is faithful and just to forgive us our sins

... wash me ... cleanse me from my sin ... lift me from the horrible pit. Restore unto me the joy of thy salvation.

Tears streamed, wetting the pillow.

—and the peace of God that passeth understanding. . . .

He slept.

In the weeks that followed, Menno lived for the letters Rachel wrote every day. He wrote her every evening, but found it difficult to express himself. His letters were awkward and stilted. He marked the thirteenth of December on the calendar in his footlocker. That was the last day of his three-month basic training, the day he would be given a furlough and would hold Rachel in his arms. Every evening he took the calendar out of the locker and crossed off another day.

A few days before the end of the training period, a sergeant, reporting the condition of his men to a superior officer, spoke with pride of the *esprit de corps* for which he seemed to take credit. He went on to explain, however, that he had one man in his outfit that he was concerned about. While the man passed with great ease all the tests of physical stamina and endurance, he failed miserably when it came to training for hand-to-hand combat, refusing to defend himself against assailants. Also, while it was hard to put a finger on it, there was something about the man's attitude that kept him separate from the other men. He was not an intregal part of the unit.

The sergeant was about to elaborate on Menno's shortcomings as a soldier and to suggest that he was not ready for combat assignment, when the officer, a frustrated stockbroker with an ulcer and a commission, cut him short with, "Send him on through! These men are not here to be pampered. Believe me, when he gets into a combat situation, and realizes those people on the other side are trying to kill him, the adrenalin will take over and he'll fight!"

"Yes, sir!" the sergeant saluted and walked away.

On the morning of December 12, Menno learned that basic

training was for ninety days, rather than three months, and because October had thirty-one days, his time was up on December 12 rather than the thirteenth. That afternoon he was on a train with a six-day furlough in his pocket.

The train pulled into the station at Newton after midnight. He decided against calling someone to pick him up. He'd wait until daylight and hitchhike home.

He passed the time pacing the floor of the waiting room, and drinking coffee in the Harvey House restaurant, which was a part of the train station. Just before sunrise he left the depot and walked north along main street. Beyond the last traffic light he left the sidewalk and began walking at the side of the street. Only two cars passed him before he reached the fork in the road where highway 81 veered off to the northwest to slice diagonally across the checkerboard squared farmland. He walked along the graveled shoulder. About a mile out of town a car stopped. The driver swung a briefcase into the back seat, making room for Menno beside him.

"Get in, soldier," he said cheerily. "Throw your bag in the back there. How far you going?"

"Just up the road a little. Prairie Ridge."

"Prairie Ridge?" The man gave a harsh laugh. "That's no place for one of Uncle Sam's finest. That place is a nest of Kraut COs."

Menno stared straight ahead. "It looks like it's going to be a nice day."

The man glanced at him sharply. "Yeah," he said.

At the edge of Prairie Ridge, Menno, indicating the crossroad ahead, asked the driver to stop. Retrieving his bag from the back seat, he said, "Thanks for the ride."

The man shrugged and sped away.

Menno began walking. About a half mile down the gravel road, a car pulled up beside him. The driver leaned over and opened the door. "Would you like a ride?" he asked, smiling. Menno got in, and held his bag on his lap. He recognized the man as a farmer from the Low German Mennonite community, but didn't remember his name.

"Say, aren't you Jonas Schrag's boy?"

Menno nodded, his mind on his meeting with his family and Rachel.

The man, in a pleasant conversational tone, said, "Guess the reason I didn't recognize you right away is I never expected to see one of Jonas Schrag's boys in an army uniform."

Menno stared straight ahead, not answering.

The man, embarrassed because he had obviously said the wrong thing, didn't speak again until he stopped at the crossroad a quarter mile from the Schrag lane. "Well, I guess this is where I go straight ahead and you turn," he said pleasantly.

"Thanks," Menno said, opening the door and getting out.

With a puzzled look, the man stared briefly at Menno's retreating figure before driving on.

Menno looked around at the familiar land as he walked quickly down the gravel road. The land on both sides of the road belonged to his family long before he was born. One quarter section was Schrag land even before his father was born. Ahead of him he saw the big, square, white house and the great red barn. The lump in his throat grew. He was at home!

He could see no signs of life around the place as he walked down the long driveway between the winter-bare cottonwoods. At the house he opened the door on the side porch and stepped into the dining room. He called out several times, and when he got no response, he realized no one was at home. In the kitchen the coffeepot was still warm. They'd probably just left for town. They weren't expecting him until tomorrow.

Outside again, he looked around. The place looked just the way he'd left it except that now it was winter. Opening the sliding door to the shed beside the granary, he saw his old black Ford, parked in its usual place. Jonas and Andy had brought it home from McPherson where he had left it. He walked around it checking the tires. They were all up, and he could find no bulges. Raising the hood, he checked the oil and the radiator. He held his nose directly over the open radiator and could smell anti-freeze. He put the cap back on and closed the hood. He dug his key out of one of the compartments in his wallet where he had put it a lifetime ago. Inserting the key into the switch and turning it, he watched the needle on the gas gauge move all the way over to "full." He pressed the starter and heard the engine turn over slowly for a few seconds before firing and coming to life. The familiar sound of the engine was one more assurance that he was at home. He backed the car out of the shed and drove to the Tobias Kaufman farm.

From the time Tim Gering had told her what he knew of Menno's experience at Fort Leavenworth, Rachel's mother, Esther, had been sympathetic. When her father, however, learned that Menno had not only disgraced himself, his family, and his church by engaging in violence, but also had actually joined the army, he announced to his family that he was never again to hear the name of Menno Schrag spoken in his house.

Rachel awoke on the morning of the thirteenth with the premonition that Menno would come today rather than tomorrow as he had written. Excited and pensive, she helped with breakfast and the packing of school lunches for the younger children. When they left for school she went back upstairs to her room, where, from her window, she could see far down the road in the direction from which Menno would be coming.

About nine o'clock Esther called up to her. "Daddy and I are going to town. We'll be back about noon."

"Okay, see you then," Rachel called back.

When they left, she was alone in the house. Her sister, two years younger than she, was away at college, the younger children were in school for the day, and Paul was doing his alternate service as an orderly in a state mental hospital in Kalamazoo, Michigan.

Rachel watched as her parents' car turned out the lane toward town. As she watched the road in the other direction, she saw Menno's black Ford. He was here! When the car began to slow down, she slipped on her coat against the cold December wind, and was out in the yard before Menno came to a stop.

She stood watching him as he slowly opened the door, got out, and hesitantly walked toward her. She ran to him and they embraced, wordlessly clinging to one another. Finally, aware of the cold, she led him to the house. Inside, they slipped out of their coats. She pulled him to the couch where they clung together again. Still no talking. That can wait. For now, holding one another, experiencing one another. A corporeal reunion of a long separated wholeness. Then the visual feasting on one another's faces, the tracing of fingers over facial features, and murmured words of love.

After a while Menno was aware that there was something different about the house, and realized that, for the first time since he had started coming to see Rachel, they were alone in the house.

"Where is everyone?" he asked.

Rachel explained.

Menno stood up and pulled her to her feet. "Let's go for a ride. I'd rather we weren't here when your dad gets back."

"Sure," she said, reaching for her coat. At the door she stopped. "I'll leave a note so they won't worry when they come back and I'm gone." Finding a sheet of paper, she wrote in large letters: "Menno is back. Gone for a ride. See you later." She laid the note on the dining room table.

Turning south at the end of the driveway, they drove for miles on the frozen dirt road. At highway 50 they turned toward Newton. They spoke little, content just being together. Most of the time Rachel's head rested on Menno's shoulder. South of Newton, on the four-lane highway to Wichita, Menno, eyes on the road, said, "I have six days. One is already gone, and it will take another one to get back. I want to be with you every minute. Let's go to Wichita and get married."

Rachel had always dreamed of her wedding day as something very different, but she was ready to settle for this. "There's a Mennonite church on Lorraine Avenue. We could go there after we get the license."

They were married that afternoon in the pastor's study, and spent the night in a hotel in downtown Wichita on Douglas Avenue.

At ten the next morning they were back at the Kaufman farm. Before the car stopped, Esther was standing on the porch shivering in the cold wind. She hadn't thought to put on her coat. As Rachel and Menno got out of the car they could see she had been crying.

"Ach Liebchen," she started crying again, "you had us so worried!"

"I'm sorry, mamma. We should have called. We were thoughtless. Come, it's cold out here." Rachel led her back into the house. Menno followed.

Inside, Tobias Kaufman, standing with his back to the table, stared at the young couple. He was pallid with rage. Finally focusing on Menno, he snarled, "You—you SOLDIER!" He put all the hatred and contempt he had into the word. "How dare you come into my house wearing that uniform! And where, in the name of common decency, have you been all night with my daughter? I will not have such filth going on in my family! You, Rachel, how do you think your mama and I and your brothers and sisters will be able to hold up our heads in church and in this community of decent people after our daughter has spent the night, only God knows where, with a soldier?"

While he was catching his breath to continue, Rachel said, "Daddy, we were married yesterday."

Tobias stood frozen, as if absorbing the shock. His anger turned cold. "If you are now the wife of a soldier, then go with your soldier!" He pointed dramatically to the door. "This is a decent Mennonite home, and we harbor no soldiers or their women!" He turned and stalked into the bedroom, firmly closing the door behind him.

"Ach, Rachel," her mother caught Rachel's hands in hers, "he didn't mean it. It's this *schrecklich°* war." Crying, she was unable to go on.

"Rachel and I will go to my house," Menno said. "She is part of my family now."

Using the hem of her apron to wipe tears from her cheeks, Esther said, "Your daddy and mama are good people. Your mama is not only my cousin, she is my friend. I'm glad Rachel will be with them."

"Would you help me get my things together?" Rachel asked her mother.

The two women went upstairs. Menno waited in the car. In a few minutes Rachel came out with only an overnight bag. As she got in the car she explained that her mother told her that her father had business at the courthouse in McPherson the next morning, and they could come for the rest of her things then.

Following the discovery of the note on the dining room table, Esther had called Anna. While Menno and Rachel were driving to the Schrag farm, Esther called Anna again. Jonas and Anna were expecting them when they drove into the yard. They hugged them both, and welcomed Rachel into the family. "With Kate married, and Marie away at college, I need another daughter," Anna said happily.

After the dinner dishes were done, the two women went upstairs and tidied up the big southwest bedroom with the brass bed and floral patterned carpet.

For the next few days the weather was cold and crisp. Each afternoon, Menno and Rachel, bundled up against the cold, walked, gloved hands clasped together, over the frozen fields. Back at the house, as the winter sun sank below the straight-lined horizon, they insisted Jonas needed a vacation, and went with Andy to the barn to help him with the chores.

° Terrible.

Menno was where he belonged. The darkness and horror of Fort Leavenworth had been pushed back until it existed only in the deepest caverns of his mind. One night, though, long after they had gone to sleep, he began to moan and thrash about. Waking, Rachel caressed him and whispered to him until the demons were put to flight. Holding her tightly to him, he fell asleep again.

The paper in the pocket of his uniform was specific. He was due back at eight-hundred hours, Monday, December 18, 1944. The date was easy to remember. It was his 26th birthday. Rising Sunday morning, he took the uniform out of the closet and put it on for the first time since coming home with Rachel.

The family took him to the Santa Fe depot in Newton for the ten o'clock train. They tried to make the ride a cheerful one for him. It was difficult for them all, knowing he would probably be sent overseas. They waited with him on the platform in front of the Harvey House restaurant. As the train pulled in, Menno gave each one a quick hug before taking Rachel into his arms again for a long good-bye kiss. He broke away, tears in his eyes, only when the conductor impatiently shouted " 'BOARD!'' for the second time.

With a great lump in his throat, he waved to Rachel and the others as the train pulled away. They would miss Sunday school, he thought, but would get to Prairie Ridge in time for the church service at eleven.

He leaned back in his seat, smiling. He had been back in the real world! A world where people loved one another. A world that was familiar and good. But, best of all, he and Rachel were man and wife! "Until death do you part," the preacher said. Somehow, what had to be endured in the next year or two, or whatever, could be endured, because he had all this to come back to.

136

12

Ten miles north of the ship, the island lay like a great, partially submerged, humpbacked, prehistoric monster. The high ridge down its center with its long line of treeless, blue-black peaks was the monster's backbone. Jungle grew like green fungus along the exposed part of the monster's great distended belly.

The men on the ship lined up along the rail, staring at the island as they headed into the blood-red sunset. Having been briefed several hours earlier, they knew this island would be their home until the army moved them elsewhere. They were being sent in as replacements for those killed or wounded.

What they were seeing was the south half of the island. Air reconnaissance had determined there were no Japanese on this side. The island, about one-hundred miles long and forty miles wide at its widest point, had no native population. The Japanese, early in the war, had occupied the northwestern section and had built an airstrip near the west end of the north shore. Army intelligence estimated the number of Japanese troops on the island at four thousand.

In October 1944, five thousand American troops landed on the beaches near the airstrip after the defenses had been softened by heavy naval bombardment. Suffering what the army considered an acceptable number of casualties, they had captured the airstrip. In six weeks they pushed the Japanese back some forty miles eastward through dense jungle to a secondary defense line they had built early in their occupation. They had built pillboxes and gun emplacements well behind the east bank of a narrow river that originated in the great central ridge, roared over a one-hundred foot cliff, and cascaded ten miles through the jungle to the sea.

The two armies faced each other across the narrow stream on a ten-mile front, with sheer, unscalable cliffs on one flank and the sea on the other. Once the Americans became entrenched on their side of the river, the firing became sporadic. The situation was a stalemate, with neither side seemingly willing nor able to break out of their entrenched position to take the offensive.

The Americans began using much of their manpower to enlarge the airport and to build a road to their front line, hauling gravel from the beaches. The men cleared a bivouac area beside the airstrip. They dug latrines, set up mess and supply tents, and tents for the officers and the enlisted men.

The supply ship carrying the replacements spent the night riding at anchor about a mile off shore, west of the airstrip. After morning mess, the men lined the rail again, watching several small craft approaching the ship from the island. One was a personnel landing craft. When it bumped up alongside the ship, the replacement men, packs on their backs, and rifles slung over their shoulders, were ordered over the side. Menno was the last one down the scramble-net into the boat.

On shore he was assigned to a small, understaffed reconnaissance platoon which was, for the time being, helping build the road to the front.

The heat and humidity were unbelievably oppressive. It rained every day. Even when it wasn't raining, the moisture-laden air was difficult to breathe. The fetid stink of death was everywhere. Breezes often stirred the treetops, but on the floor of the jungle there was no movement of air. The men moved about sluggishly, the oppressive heat dulling their minds and bodies.

On his first day on the road job, Menno remembered that it

was the middle of January. If he were at home, he could possibly be walking to the barn through snowdrifts, head down against the northwest wind. A wave of homesickness swept over him.

While there were seldom more than a third of the enlisted men and noncoms at the front in battle readiness at any given time, all who did not have permanent jobs at island head-quarters took their turns relieving those at the front lines. Menno's platoon had just come off the line the day before he arrived. He knew that, sooner or later, he would be in a foxhole or a trench, expected to help repulse an attack or help launch one.

Some of the men in his platoon talked among themselves of their experiences. This was their second campaign. At the be-ginning of their first they had been at full strength. When Menno was assigned to them, they were down to ten men. He felt they resented him as an outsider, ignorant of the horrors and indignities they had shared.

The platoon consisted of two squads, each led by a buck sergeant. One of them was named Shapiro. During a work break, which the men took frequently in the stifling heat, Shapiro, a man about Menno's age, asked him where he was from and what he did in civilian life. Several of the men over-heard him say he was a farmer from Kansas. He was thereafter called Farmer. Few bothered to learn his real name.

The road building had progressed to a point very near the front. Periodically shells exploded in the jungle nearby. Menno winced at each one, but the others appeared not to notice.

A couple of trucks dumped more gravel. For a while the men busied themselves leveling it, extending the roadbed a few feet. Menno noticed that the smell of rotting flesh had become stronger. A nineteen-year-old with acne scars and jungle sores on his face approached Menno. He spoke with a west-side New York City Accent, and was called McGinty. "Hey, Farmer, wanna see somptin?" He motioned Menno to follow him into the jungle. Menno looked at Shapiro questioningly. Shapiro

139

shrugged. Menno followed the young man on a narrow path, doubling over to avoid vines and branches. The stench of rotting flesh became unbearable. About thirty yards from the road, Menno, bent over to avoid a vine, bumped into McGinty who had stopped. Menno straightened up and, looking over McGinty's shoulder, saw they had come to a small clearing about thirty feet across. McGinty stepped aside. Lying on the floor of the clearing were the rotting corpses of six Japanese soldiers. Menno stared in transfixed horror. The contorted bodies lay where the exploding grenade had left them. Two lay face down and four were on their backs. Their bodies had swollen until their uniforms were ready to burst. Two of them had had their bellies torn open. The large holes were filled with shimmering masses of slimy, frantically burrowing maggots. The corpses whose faces were exposed, stared at the sky from eye sockets being emptied by squirming maggots. Mouths, voraciously open, were filled to overflowing with the hungry larva. Big green flies heavy with eggs buzzed over the corpses, looking for more exposed flesh.

"Friggin' Jap patrol sneaked over da river night 'fore last. Chavez, he seen 'em an' lobs a friggin' grenade right smack in da middle of 'em. Dat fixed 'em, but good!"

Menno turned and retched.

> And God said, let us make man in our own image, after our own likeness. So God created man in his own image, in the image of God created he him.

Regaining control of his convulsing stomach, Menno straightened up. McGinty was gone. Finding the trail, Menno made his way back to the road. McGinty was talking to some of the younger men. They looked at Menno out of the corners of their eyes, suppressing grins. Shapiro, leaning on his shovel some distance from the others, glanced at Menno and quickly looked away.

That evening Lieutenant Charles Glover was summoned to

Major General Reid's tent. Glover, who had been assigned to ordnance since the start of the campaign, was pleasantly surprised to learn that he was being placed in charge of a small reconnaissance platoon and would be sent on a mission the next day.

Maps spread out on his desk, Reid explained the nature of the mission and its importance. The recon platoon was to be taken in an assault boat to the middle of the south shore. They would disembark and proceed through the jungle and the grasslands of the upper slopes to a specific pass through the central ridge. Once through the pass, they would carefully proceed through the jungle again, this time behind enemy lines. Because of the density of the jungle, air reconnaissance was not able to give a clear picture of the strength of the enemy nor of its specific emplacements.

Their mission was not only to bring back a report of the strength and emplacements of the enemy, but to verify a route over which troops could be moved for an attack on the enemy's rear, mounted simultaneously with a frontal attack across the stream. The navy had promised cooperation with a coordinated bombardment.

The next morning the men of the platoon were told to prepare their equipment and packs for an extended reconnaissance mission. Lieutenant Glover had spent the time previous to the launching procuring the boat and pilot, checking all equipment and supplies, and going over maps and charts to familiarize himself with the terrain they must cross. Unfamiliar with the men he was to lead, he received permission to examine the files of each one. Listing their names on a sheet of paper, he made notations after each name in his own form of shorthand that would tell him something about each man's record and background.

When all was ready, he had the men assemble before him on the edge of the beach. Standing on the lowered ramp of the assault boat, he called out each man's name, motioning them forward into the craft. He studied them carefully as they walked by him, to associate the name with the man.

The pilot took the boat about a mile out from shore before turning parallel to it. The flat-bottomed craft rolled and pitched as it moved slowly over the choppy water. The lieutenant stood in the pilot's hatch at the rear. Pretending to be checking details of the mission as he glanced from time to time at the paper in his hand, he was in reality rechecking the names on his list and studying the men.

He had been told that, with one exception, they had all been through two campaigns together and had acquitted themselves well. The new man was one of the replacements just out from stateside. Coming directly from basic training, his value to the mission was a toss-up. One thing in his favor, at twenty-six, he wasn't a kid. Also, in civilian life he was a farmer, so he could probably take care of himself in wilderness country.

Sergeant Shapiro's file indicated he had a college degree. It will be good to have someone to talk to, but then you always had to be careful talking to Jews. You never knew, until it was too late, when they were going to take offense. Intelligent Jews were okay, but they were such touchy bastards. The Mexican from El Paso, Chavez, was a small man who smiled a lot, wanting to please. A good Mex who knew his place. He moved with the grace of a cat. He'd do okay on the mission. Jackson. Southern Appalachian hillbilly, built like an ox. Probably completely illiterate, but strength and endurance could go a long way on this mission.

Continuing through the list, Glover tried to assess the value of each man to the mission. He was bothered by the fact that he had never led a recon platoon before, and that some of the men were probably better qualified for his job than he was.

He lit another cigarette and went down into the crowded troop well. Trying to appear casual, he made small talk with the men. He made a point of speaking each man's name while addressing him. He wanted to be liked, but was aware that an officer must, of necessity, keep a certain distance between himself and his men.

As the red sun sank to the horizon, reflecting eerily on the blue-black peaks, black clouds began roiling up in the east. The men fell silent, staring alternately at the sinking sun, the rolling, threatening clouds, and the humpbacked island, brooding over the green undulating sea. No one thought of giving it words, but each man sensed an evil force emanating from the island.

A few minutes after sundown, the island disappeared in darkness. Twilight at this latitude is short-lived.

The men settled down on their cots hoping to get some sleep. In about an hour the rain started. One minute there was no rain, and the next, torrents poured over them, lashing at the ponchos they huddled under. Hour after hour, in the black night, the rain pounded them. Everything in the boat not encased in rubber was saturated. Sometime after midnight the rain eased up, stopping completely sometime before the silhouette of the island became visible against the low, scudding clouds. Dawn, like the twilight, was short. In a few minutes the sun, a red, luminous balloon, popped out of the sea. The clouds disappeared into the west, and the dark peaks stood out against the brilliant blue sky. The green, rain-wet jungle glistened and sparkled in the bright morning sun.

The boat headed for the beach. When the ramp was let down, the men, glad to be off the cramped, wet boat, walked about on the wide, pebbly beach. A fresh breeze came in off the sea from the southeast. It was pleasantly cool.

The assault craft backed away and started its return trip. It was to return for them in five days. The jungle sounds, silenced by the unaccustomed noise of the engines, started again. Birds called raucously, and monkeys chattered in the treetops. The many sounds the men couldn't identify were simply thought of as jungle sounds.

While the men walked slowly about on the beach, letting the morning sun dry their clothes, Glover spread a map on the sand, and called Shapiro and Kawalski, the two sergeants, for consultation.

"It looks like the best way up is to work our way up that river as far as we can." He pointed to a stream pouring out of the jungle some yards east of them. "The map shows the jungle only about three miles wide here. It's hard to tell from an aerial map, but it looks like the area between the jungle and the divide is covered with grass.

"Dem aerial maps ain't too dependable. Few feet back from da beach it don't show no river. Friggin' trees cover it right over. Maybe it'll take us where we wanna go, maybe not," Kawalski said in his staccato Chicago-Slavic accent.

"Well there's only one way to find out. Get the men together and let's go in."

Turning to the men, Kawalski said authoritatively, "Okay yous men, look alive dere, we're goin' in."

Gathered at the mouth of the river, they stopped while Glover addressed them. "I want you men to know we are beginning a difficult assignment. We are not only going to go through difficult terrain, but, air recon over jungle country being what it is, we have no guarantees there are no Japs on this side of the island. We have to be alert at all times for possible ambush or snipers. You men have been together on dangerous missions before, so I don't have to tell you the value of working together as a team. Remember, no matter how tough the going gets, stay alert at all times." Turning, he stepped into the river where it emerged from the jungle. He hoped his little speech and the way he delivered it helped dispel any doubts the men may have had about his leadership.

Adjusting their packs and rifles, the men fell in behind one another, entering the stream in a single column. Deep in the middle, the stream was shallow with a pebbly bottom along both sides. Very quickly it narrowed and the men found themselves in a tunnel. The jungle had closed over their heads, shutting out the sun. The little light that filtered through produced a dark green haze that was palpable. They were engulfed in the sounds and smells of the jungle. The cloying sweetness of tropical flowers, the wet, pungent smell of newly emerging

144

plants burgeoning out of the decay on the jungle floor, the overpowering stench of death and decay filled their senses, stalking them with an undefined horror.

"Hit shore do stink," Jackson said, glancing uneasily about him.

The stream twisted and curved its way into the jungle. Already the men had forgotten what the sunlight and fresh air was like on the beach. Their ears were filled with the frenetic buzzing of insects, and the raucous chattering and babbling of jungle birds and monkeys. The languid air gave them no nourishment. Their breath came in gasps. The growing heat of the unseen sun turned the water on the rain-soaked foliage into mist which parted for their passage and closed again behind their bodies. Their clothing was saturated from sweat, mist, and the dripping ceiling of the dark green tunnel. Every step demanded an effort of will. They stopped often to catch their breath, shivering with revulsion.

The stream became narrower and the men were often forced to walk in the deeper water which soaked through their boots, sloshing about and galling their feet. Their arms grew numb and their backs began to ache from the weight of their packs, rifles, and extra ammunition and equipment hanging from their shoulders and belts.

By the time they had struggled a mile, mind dulling fatigue replaced their initial revulsion and terror. In spite of Glover's lecture, they began to look at their boots as they laboriously and painfully put one in front of the other.

The stream narrowed again and the water was deep from bank to bank. They had been climbing steadily from the start, but now the stream was a torrent, rushing at them from above. Waist deep in the turbulent water, the men had to cling to vines and branches overhanging the bank in order to keep their footing. The gravel stream bed became deep, boot-sucking mud. They pulled themselves along inch by inch, forgetting, momentarily, their fatigue in their anxiety. The rushing water was powerful and malevolent, filling them with dread. Their hands began to bleed from the thorny vines and branches.

The stream widened again after a time, and they were able to slosh through knee-deep water. At another turn they came to a huge, flat rock at the side of the stream. Glover called a break. Slipping off their packs, the men lay on their backs, glad to be out of the water. After about five minutes most of the men sat up, conversing among themselves, speculating on what lay ahead.

Menno sat, partially turned away from the others, and stared at the rushing water. As usual he was thinking of home. Jackson, sitting about six feet away, hitched closer. Menno glanced at him, smiled, and looked back at the water.

"Thet there water's shor in a par'ful hurry teh git teh thet there ocean."

"Yeah."

Jackson looked at Menno speculatively. "You don't never cuss like them other uns, nor talk dirty. You got religion?"

Menno looked at him and smiled. He shrugged. "Yeah, I guess you could say that."

"Baptist?"

"No, I'm a Mennonite."

"Never heerd tell o' such. I reckon you all b'lieve in Jesus an' all thet?"

"Yes."

"My maw, she's powerful religious, she says Missionary Baptists has got hit right, but she allows as how all them others, if'n they b'lieve in Jesus, why the Lord's gonna take 'em in even if'n they aint got everythin' quite right." He was quiet for a moment. "Got saved an' baptized when ah wan't mor'n a tyke. Went teh preachin' reg'ler. Then ah jined th' army an' got teh drinkin an' a'whorin' 'roun'. Reckon ah ain't saved no more." He reflected a moment. " 'Tain't like them Hardshell Baptists, claimin' thet onc't yeh git saved yeh c'n do anythin' yeh've a mind teh an' yeh won't never go teh hell. No sir, hit jist hain't thet way atall."

"All right, men," the lieutenant called. The men struggled to

their feet. Menno put his hand on Jackson's shoulder for a
second, smiling at him. The men slipped on their packs and
followed Glover into the stream. Jackson stayed close to
Menno's side.

They began climbing a series of cascades. Coming around a
bend, they almost lost their footing when they were hit by the
force of the water coming through a huge flume. Pulling themselves along the vertical clay bank, they struggled against the
current, hanging on to slippery roots protruding from the bank.
They became covered with sticky, blue clay as they clung to
the bank on the side of the flume. Once through the narrow,
steep defile, the stream leveled again. The men struggled
through shallower water, sinking deeply into the soft, muddy
stream bed. They were becoming very tired. Some had lost a
degree of control over their limbs, occasionally floundering as
their knees buckled.

A hundred yards upstream they came to a rapids, steeper,
longer, and more vicious than the clay-banked flume. With
awesome power, the water roared toward them over and
around great boulders. Glover stopped to study the situation.
In a moment he signaled Shapiro, and the two men scrambled
up the bank. Hacking their way a few feet into the jungle, they
cut a number of long, ropelike vines. The men helped pull the
vines into the stream, tying them together with square knots.
Tying one end around his waist, Glover started up the rapids.
The men stared after him as he made his way from boulder to
boulder. Hesitating on the top of each one, he studied the next
one, looking for fingerholds and toeholds. Each effort called for
reserves of strength he didn't know he had. Reaching the top,
he staggered to the bank, collapsing against a tree. As he tied
the end of the vine around the tree, his breath came in great
wrenching sobs. He knew he had not only conquered the
rapids but had established himself as the leader of the platoon.
Sitting on the bank, boots in the stream, he raised his hand,
signaling the men to come up.

Carrying Glover's pack and carbine, as well as his own,

Shapiro was the first to grasp the vine and begin to pull himself up. "Now there's a Mensch!" he said to himself.

One by one the men pulled themselves up the rapids and sat down in the shallow water near the bank gasping for air. In about fifteen minutes Glover stood up and resumed the climb. The men lethargically got to their feet to follow. The stream bed was now, for the most part, solid rock. The water cascaded over shelves of flat rocks, each of which was only one or two feet lower than the one above. Slowly, in single file, the men climbed the stairlike stream through the narrow, low-ceilinged tunnel. Each time they saw a tiny stream emptying into the main one, they were aware that the stream was becoming smaller. Finally they were crawling on their hands and knees up the yard-wide stream, when the jungle closed over them completely. They had come to the point where the water was flowing toward them from several directions in tiny rivulets originating in springs bubbling out of the sloping jungle floor. They had reached the source of the stream. When the line came to a halt, the men in the rear didn't know what was happening, but were glad for the respite.

At the head of the line, Glover began slashing with his machete until he had cleared a large enough space for several men to stand up. Shapiro joined him. Standing back to back, slashing away at the vines and brush, they soon had a large enough area cleared so that all the men could cluster together in the clearing. Consulting a map which he took out of a rubber pouch in his pack, Glover addressed the men. "Even though I took frequent compass readings while winding our way up here, I can't say for an absolute certainty, but we should be close to a straight line between the place where we started and the pass over the ridge we're headed for. I figure we have about a mile to go before we get out of this jungle and into grassland. We'll break out some rations now and get a little nourishment. Then we'll start cutting trail. Two men will work together for five minutes, drop back to rest and two others will be ready to take their place. We'll work that way through the whole platoon and then start over again. A few more hours and we'll see daylight." He looked at his watch. It was twelve o'clock. They had covered about two miles in five and a half hours.

By dividing into two-man teams, working five minutes at a time, the men were able to rest long enough between work stints to regain some of their strength. Large trees and heavy clusters of giant bamboo were circumvented, so the trail was by no means straight. Frequent compass readings, however, kept the winding trail fairly well on course.

Cutting through the jungle took longer than Glover had anticipated. It was five-thirty when the last team of slashers finally broke through into the daylight. Menno was working with Jackson, and they walked out of the jungle together. Having always lived on the open plains of Kansas, the jungle had been a nightmare for Menno. Many times in the stifling tunnel of the upper part of the stream and the narrow, slashed trail he fought off the terror of claustrophobia. Now, even though the sounds of the jungle were still in his ears, its stink still in his nostrils, and he still had to gasp to breathe the heavy, fetid air, he could see a distant horizon. He felt like a drowning man feels when he is pulled from the water.

The men all filed out of the jungle and stood blinking in the sunlight. It seemed an eon ago that they had seen the rays of the morning sun silver-dappling the swells of the rolling sea. Now, through the face-high grass around them, they saw the sun sinking in the western sky.

Glover led the men through a deep ravine to the crest of a ridge running parallel to the jungle's edge, where he could get a better look at the great ridge with its peaks and passes. Consulting his aerial map again, he was satisfied they had come through the jungle with the least possible deviation from their course. Aerial maps, however, were unreliable in that they invariably showed the land beneath the plane to be flat. The grassland between the jungle and the island's backbone was actually rugged terrain with choppy hills and deep gullies. The

149

map also gave no indication of the tremendous height of the grass.

While Glover looked over the terrain yet to be covered, the men flopped down around him, completely exhausted. When it began suddenly to get dark, they roused themselves enough to break out some rations and unpack their blankets and ponchos for the night. Some were too tired to eat, and drank a little from their canteens.

Menno lay on his back looking at the stars. The night sky was different than in Kansas. Nowhere could he find either the Big or Little Dipper. Looking over the top of the jungle, he saw stars lined up in the form of a huge cross. Numb with fatigue, he began to drift into sleep.

> I will cling to the old rugged cross,
> And exchange it some day for a crown.

13

About midnight it began to rain again. The men huddled, miserable and wet, under their ponchos. It rained hard for about two hours, eased up, and quit entirely before dawn. Glover, up at first light, woke the sergeants, who, in turn, shook their men awake. The rain had saturated the clay soil so that the men sank to their ankles at each step. The thick, head-high grass shook water on them at their every movement, so that by the time they were ready to resume the march, they were wet to the skin.

The slow march continued through the day. The clouds disappeared soon after sunup. As the morning progressed the heat became more oppressive. The sun bore down on them unmercifully while steam from the saturated soil and grass made the air heavy to breathe. The wet clay clung to their boots, adding pounds to their weight. By now most of the men had big blisters on their feet, some of which were beginning to fester. After crossing a broad valley, they began to climb over steep ridges, each one higher than the last, as they climbed toward the island's great, jagged spinal column. The hills were so steep the men grasped the stems of the tall grass to pull themselves up. The sharp blades of the coarse grass cut their hands and faces. At the top of each hill they flopped to the wet ground, gasping for breath. After a few minutes they were ordered on their feet again, and the trek continued. The nearer they got to the great ridge, the more they considered the possibility of an enemy ambush. Anxiety was added to their fatigue and pain.

The grass was shorter at the higher altitude, and Glover ordered the men to bend over and keep a low profile as they crossed the ridges. The soil was becoming stony, and rock outcroppings began to appear. Ahead of them were clumps of bushes surrounded by short grass. The ridges no longer ran parallel to the spinal column, but at right angles to it, as the land began to rise sharply toward the base of the great jagged peaks that were the primordial vertebrae of the island's spine.

Glover led the column into the low end of a deep ravine, the top of which pointed directly upward toward their goal. He estimated they were about two miles from the pass. At the top of the ravine they should be no more than a mile and a half from the deep declevity between two of the peaks through which they would go to reach the north slope and their destination.

The steep ravine was strewn with large blue-black boulders. The men spaced themselves about five yards apart as they cautiously wound their way upward around the boulders and scattered bushes. The sun on their left was too low in the early evening sky to shine into the ravine, but its rays could still be seen on the ridge on their right where a few trees grew out of the rocky soil.

The higher the men climbed the more apprehensive they became. Everyone suspected the Japanese were guarding the pass, and could very well have patrols on the south slope. The nearer they came to the divide, the greater the danger. At a narrow, particularly steep point in the ravine, Menno glanced ahead and to his right at a tree on the bank. Through the foliage he caught the glint of sunlight on steel. A rifle barrel was pointed directly at Jackson, who was behind him in the column. Menno reacted automatically. As he screamed "No!" he threw his rifle toward the sniper, not thinking of it as a weapon but as an object to be used to divert the malicious intent of the man in the tree. At the same instant he threw the rifle, he leaped protectingly between the pointed weapon and

152

its target. The bullet entered his abdomen just to the right of his navel. A volley of rifle shots echoed through the ravine. Menno sat on the ground staring at the tree. The sniper's rifle fell to the ground, then slowly, head first, his riddled body slid through the branches and fell in a crumpled heap, covering his weapon.

An eerie silence filled the ravine. The men were all lying, prone and tense, behind boulders or bushes. Menno sat staring at the crumpled, contorted body. In a state of acute shock, he was unable to understand what had happened. Had he been kicked in the stomach? He rubbed his hand over it. His stomach was wet and sticky. Slowly he brought his hand up and saw blood dripping from his fingers. He stared at the dripping blood.

> What can wash away my sins?
> Nothing but the blood of Jesus.

His eyes rolled upward as the lids closed over them. Collapsing on his backpack, he rolled toward the middle of the ravine until his pack stopped him and he lay still.

The silence continued for several more minutes while the men considered whether this had been a lone sniper or a member of a nearby patrol that would attack at any moment. When no movement or sound was observed, Glover decided the man, for some reason, was alone. The sound of shots, however, would have carried to the pass, and if it was being guarded, as he suspected, they could shortly expect an investigating patrol. They must move fast.

Before entering the ravine he had noted a huge field of boulders, starting at the ravine and extending several miles eastward. The rocky ground would leave no tracks, and the boulders would offer protection if they were attacked.

After removing Menno's backpack, four men carried him to the rim of the ravine, while another man carried his pack. The platoon ran through the field of boulders bending over to avoid detection. Every few hundred yards another team of four would take over and carry Menno. About four miles east they came to a cluster of boulders in the middle of a large gravel slide, offering a clear view on all sides. Glover decided this would be a good defensive position and called a halt. The sun had set, and daylight was rapidly fading.

In the morning they would continue eastward and cross over through the next pass. It was much farther behind the Japanese lines, but was less likely to be guarded.

Before the darkness was complete, he ordered two of the men to cut some poles from a clump of small trees a hundred yards up the slope. They were to use their knives, whittling the small trees from their stumps. The sound of chopping could not be risked. In the now almost total darkness Glover and Shapiro used the poles, along with a blanket and several belts, to make a stretcher.

Four guards were posted throughout the night. About midnight Menno slowly regained consciousness. At first he thought he was in bed at home and had awakened with a stomach ache. What had he eaten that would make his stomach hurt like this? He heard two men whispering beside him. Little by little it came back to him. The sunlight on the rifle, the kick in the stomach, the body falling from the tree. He sat up quickly, flailing his arms and shouting "I can't see!"

"Hey, take it easy, Farmer. It's the middle of the night. It's dark, that's why you can't see." Dimly Menno saw Shapiro's face close to his. Looking at him uncertainly, he lay back down. He must have been asleep. The sun was shining, and now it's dark. His stomach hurt. No one had kicked him. It was that rifle in the tree. There was a hole in his belly. He put his hand to his abdomen. Someone had taken away his belt. There was a bandage over his stomach. He remembered. There was a hole. Rachel would say, "Why, Menno, you have two belly buttons! Don't you think one is enough?" He began to chuckle. There was blood in his mouth.

Blood.... There is power, wonder-working power in the blood

154

of the Lamb.... When the angel of death sees blood on the doorposts, he passes over you.... Without the shedding of blood there is no remission of sin.... There is a fountain filled with blood, drawn from Immanuel's veins.... This cup is the new testament in my blood.... Whoso eateth and drinketh my blood hath eternal life.... Are your garments spotless? Are they white as snow? Are you washed in the blood of the Lamb?

Unconscious through the rest of the night, Menno slowly wrestled his way back to consciousness. He felt himself being jostled. He wanted to see what was happening, but when he tried to open his eyes, the sun was too bright. Little by little he pried them open. Two men with packs on their backs were plodding along. They seemed to be pulling him feet first, behind them. Twisting his head, he saw two more men behind him. He was being carried through a cane field.

Andy! Andy! The cows are in the cane field! We gotta get 'em outa there before they eat too much of it and bloat! Come on! Let's go!

The searing pain in his belly made him want to scream. He clamped his jaws together and moaned. The pain and nausea were too much for his mind to accept and he sank back into oblivion.

Hour after hour the men struggled through the tall grass. Not a breath of air stirred. The tropical sun bore down on them without mercy. They gulped the heavy fetid air into their lungs and were not nourished by it. On the downward slope of steep hills they often stumbled, the stretcher hitting the ground hard. Menno moaned and thrashed about. Getting to their feet, the men would lurch forward gasping and sobbing for air that seared their throats and hurt their lungs.

Menno wandered in and out of consciousness. His wound throbbed. The pain was excruciating. Each jolt of the stretcher was like the shock of a blow.

About one o'clock, the two men in the rear, Jennings and Watts, stumbled, dropped their end of the stretcher, and pitched forward on their faces. Menno screamed with pain and

155

passed out again. Shapiro and Jackson eased their end of the stretcher to the ground. They lay on their backs. The four men lay gasping and sobbing for air, their bodies trembling with exhaustion.

Lying still, Menno worked his way by degrees, back to consciousness again. The lower part of his body had become numb, and he felt scarcely any pain. He was, however, aware of a terrible stench. Nausea had caused him to vomit, soaking the blanket around his head. His thrashing about had loosened the bandage on his wound. Intestinal fluid as well as blood, was continually oozing from his wound, saturating his clothing and the stretcher blanket. Without his being aware of it, his bowels had voided, adding to the stench. He lay watching the great green flies buzzing languidly over him.

After half an hour the men were breathing easier. Jackson was up first, then Shapiro struggled to his feet. The jungle sores on his feet had ruptured. He could feel blood squishing in his boots. They had to pull Jennings and Watts to their feet. Grumbling and cursing, they picked up their end of the stretcher.

They struggled on, setting their burden down every two or three hundred yards for a short rest. Within a few hundred yards of the jungle, Watts collapsed. Jennings lay down beside him. After a fifteen-minute rest, Shapiro said, "We have to keep going men. Lieutenant Glover entrusted us with this mission so that he and the rest of the men could complete the job we were sent here to do. It won't take nearly as long to go back through the jungle as it did coming up through it. If we start now, we could be on the beach before dark."

"We ain't goin' no place," Jennings said.

"Whata ya mean?" Jackson asked, alarmed, "We gotta git this man down to the beach! Why he done saved mah life. Why he jumps right out fronta me an' takes that there bullit afore hit could git me raht inna chest. 'Twern't fer him, ah'm tellin' ya, ah'd be raht smack in hell raht now."

"Aw don't be so friggin dumb, you hillbilly bastard. You'd

156

be layin' dead up there in the ravine. There ain't no such place as hell," Jennings said scornfully.

"Now thet jist hain't raht! No sir. This man hadna stop thet there bullit fer me, ah'd be a'roastin' inna flames raht now! He done saved me. This here man's mah frien', mah buddy."

"Come on men, get on your feet and let's go. We'll be on the beach before dark." Shapiro tried to sound authoritative.

"Watts an' me ain't goin' nowhere, you friggin' Jew-Kike-Sheeny-Hebe bastard."

Well, I guess that's what it always comes down to, Shapiro thought. Slipping off his backpack he laid it on the ground, carefully laying his rifle on it. He signaled Jackson to do the same. "You men bring these down when you come," he said, lifting one end of the stretcher. Jackson picked up the other end. The two men staggered with their burden toward the tunnel through the jungle.

Beyond pain, Menno was lethargic. Idly, he touched his hand to his wound. When it came away, several tiny white maggots clung to his fingers. He brushed them off on the side of the stretcher.

And though after my skin worms destroy this body, yet in my flesh shall I see God.

Great green flies swarmed and buzzed over the wound.

Alle Menschen müssen sterben;
alles Fleisch ist gleich wie Heu;
was da lebet, muss verderben,
soll es anders werden neu.°

The men found the entrance to the tunnel and pulled the stretcher into the darkness of the jungle. Menno imagined himself a small child again, about to go to sleep in his warm bed.

°See page 238.

Müde bin ich, geh zur Ruh,
schliesse meine Augen zu;
Vater, lass die Augen dein
über meinem Bette sein.°

The trail made by the platoon was narrow and winding. It was hard for Shapiro and Jackson to drag the stretcher through it. Menno was not aware of his surroundings again until the men were forced to put the stretcher down into the water after they had reached the upper part of the stream. The water flowing around his body felt good. In a few minutes the men staggered to their feet again. The water was flowing over shelves of flat rock. The stream widened, the water was deeper, flowing faster.

The dark green tunnel and the stream had been loathsome and terrifying to Menno on the way up. Now it was strangely benign, friendly, seeming to beckon to him.

Ich weiss einem Strom, dessen herrliche Flut
fliesst wunderbar stille durchs Land,°°

As the water deepened, the men were too exhausted to lift their burden above it. Often only Menno's head was above water. He became euphoric, increasingly aware of a joyous anticipation deep within him. The dark tunnel had become suffused with light and color, luminous and shining.

Suddenly he was aware that, far below him, two men were toiling in the water, carrying a third man between them. The men seemed not to see the approaching rapids until they were swept into it. Menno watched as they were tossed about like corks, sometimes totally submerged. At the bottom of the rapids, the two men struggled to their feet, still clutching the handles of the stretcher. Carefully they continued picking their

---

° See page 238.
°° I know a stream, this powerful flood flows wonderfully quiet through the land.

way through the swiftly flowing water, too numb from exhaustion to see that their stretcher was empty.

And the golden light became white and pure and all encompassing. The morning stars sang together, and the sons of God shouted for joy, while the music of the spheres beckoned from beyond the astral plains.

Part Three

MICHAEL
1967-1968

14

The great green tractor roared across the south quarter section, adding another broad ribbon of black clodded soil to the already wide strip of plowed ground started that morning near the south end of the half-mile-square field. By ten o'clock the hot sun was bearing down on the land, reflecting shimmering heat waves over the thick yellow wheat stubble. The green osage orange hedges which bordered the field appeared to be dancing in the sun.

Michael, sitting comfortably on the wide, cushioned seat in the air-conditioned cab, guided the tractor from one end of the field to the other, oblivious to the intense heat outside. The roar of the great diesel engine was only a subdued, background hum. Michael's ears were covered with earphones plugged into his tape deck. He was listening to the Beatles.

His Uncle Andy, working with the old tractor today, was plowing in the field across the road. A huge orange umbrella, bolted to the tractor's right fender, protected him from the sun.

When Michael reached the end of the field, he power-steered the tractor sharply to the right, selected a small lever from a row of identical ones beside the armrest, and pushed it a few inches forward. This activated a hydraulic cylinder that raised the semi-mounted plow out of the ground. He swung the tractor back into the furrow on the other side of the strip of plowed land, and dropped the plow into the ground again with an almost effortless adjustment.

George Harrison was singing, "Here comes the sun."

As the tractor pulled back and forth across the field, changing the color of the land from yellow to black, Michael gave only part of his attention to the taped music, letting his mind wander where it would. He was intrigued by the new tractor. His Uncle Andy, anticipating a good wheat crop, had bought just before harvest. He kept the old one too, reasoning that the more horsepower he had working for him, the less work he would have to do.

The old tractor had little more than half the horsepower of the new one, so the previous summer Michael and his uncle had kept the tractor and plow going day and night. There would be no need this year to plow at night.

The air conditioned cab, fingertip controls, and taped music made plowing so easy and pleasurable, Michael felt guilty letting his uncle pay him. He decided, however, that he could live with the guilt. He needed the money for tuition and living expenses at the university, and even though his '66 Mustang was paid for, it took money to drive it.

Looking out over the broad, level fields, and at the neat farmstead with its big, square house, red barn, shady yard, and cottonwood-tree-lined driveway, he realized how much he loved the place. It had been his only home until he was almost seventeen. His mother, Rachel, had remarried that summer, and his stepfather Roy had accepted a job as a design engineer for a farm equipment manufacturer in Michigan.

His stepfather was his father's cousin and had been a bachelor until he was forty. After having earned a degree in agricultural engineering, he returned to his family's farm and formed a partnership with his younger brother. Both parents died young, and the two brothers had lived alone for many years. When the younger brother married in his early thirties and began to raise a family, Roy sold his share of the farm to his brother and looked for employment as an engineer.

At the same time he also began to think seriously of marriage. He had known Rachel all his life, and that summer he

164

persuaded her to share her life with him. She quit her job at the bank in Prairie Ridge, and they were married. Two weeks later they were getting settled in their new home in Holland, Michigan.

At first Michael had insisted on staying on the family farm in Kansas. His mother was just as insistent that he go with them to Michigan. They finally reached a compromise and Michael agreed to go with them if he could spend his summers in Kansas.

The day after graduating from high school the next spring, Michael was on his way back to Kansas. The following September he was in Michigan again, starting classes at Western Michigan University in Kalamazoo. Later that month, on his eighteenth birthday, he registered for the draft in the town of Holland.

He liked the term system newly instituted at Western. The fall and winter terms were for sixteen weeks each, and the spring and summer terms were eight-week periods. He enrolled only for the fall and winter terms so that he could spend four months each year on the farm in Kansas.

During the fall of 1966 and the winter of 1967, he let his hair and beard grow. His wavy, light brown hair hung to his shoulders, and his well-trimmed beard, along with his widely spaced blue eyes, gave him the appearance of a Renaissance painting of Christ. He was concerned that his relatives in "middle America" might label him a "hippie," and be offended by his appearance. He need not have worried. On his first Sunday in church that spring, he saw that several of his friends from the Mennonite college in Newton were wearing long hair and beards.

At the dinner table that Sunday Andy Schrag commented, "When I was a kid all the old men in church wore beards, and all the young men shaved. Now it's the other way around."

"Why don't you grow a beard?" Michael asked. "I think you'd look very distinguished."

Andy laughed, "If I'd start growing a beard people would

say I was trying to recapture my misspent youth by trying to look like a college kid. I'm afraid I'm stuck with having to scrape my face every morning for the rest of my life."

Michael smiled, remembering the conversation.

At noon he pushed the little lever forward and the plow sprang out of the ground. He shifted into road-gear and the tractor raced toward the house. When he pulled up to the fuel pump under the big elm tree in the backyard, he was greeted by Brownie, the family collie, who stood panting and wagging his tail. Early in the morning the dog had followed Andy as he plowed with the old tractor back and forth across the field. Now, in the midday heat, he rested in the shade, his tongue dripping.

Michael stopped the engine and climbed out of the cab. His sixteen-year-old cousin, David, greased the plow while Michael serviced the tractor, filling the fuel tank and checking the oil level in the crankcase and transmission.

David was mechanically inclined and had very quickly learned to operate the new tractor. He had eaten an early lunch so that he could take the tractor back to the field to keep it going while Michael had lunch with his Aunt Sarah and fourteen-year-old Peter.

At one o'clock Michael drove the pickup truck to the field and resumed plowing. David took the truck back to the house. When he got there his father brought the old tractor in from the west eighty. David took it back to the field to plow after he and his father serviced it. He plowed for an hour while Andy ate lunch.

About three o'clock three jets, flying in formation, streaked their silver lines across the pale blue sky from east to west. Michael followed them until they became tiny specks in the distance and then disappeared. Probably on their way to "bomb the Vietnamese back into the stone age." Grandmothers in their rocking chairs and mothers clutching their children blown to bits so that communism would be contained and no more dominoes would fall. Bombers flying over Kansas wheat fields on their way to support our gallant troops on the ground while they machine-gunned and burned villages, and tonight CBS will give us the body count. Thirty-nine American and five hundred known communist casualties.

Strange how they always know that all the Vietnamese dead are communists.... Probably clutching copies of *Das Kapital* in their dead hands. Maybe they have party membership cards in their pockets ... or pinned to their diapers.

Michael felt a familiar tightening in his gut.

As he headed east he saw Dan Graber plowing his quarter section across the road. Michael wondered what Deacon Dan thought about as he sat watching the furrow in front of him. Did he feel outrage over the atrocities committed in Vietnam in the name of the American people? If so he did a good job of concealing it. Last Sunday during Sunday school hour, when Art Wedel read his paper on civil disobedience and passive resistance, and Sam Waltner stood up to say the church should support the anti-war demonstrations of the students, old Deacon Dan got up and started talking about how we Mennonites have always been '*die Stillen im Land*'° and we shouldn't rock the boat, and the United States of America has been good to us, letting our young men do alternate service, and if America hadn't taken us in we'd still be in Russia where we'd be living under godless communism and, after all, our government is doing what it can to protect us from communism, and if we make trouble our young men could lose their special status as consciencious objectors.

As usual everybody sat and thought about this awhile. Then banker John J. C. stood and in his smooth-as-silk voice read from Romans: "Let every soul be subject unto the higher powers, for there is no power but of God: the powers that be are ordained of God. Whosoever therefore resisteth the power, resisteth the ordinance of God: and they that resist shall receive unto themselves damnation."

° The quiet in the land.

167

Art turned red and was about to defend the ideas in his paper when old Botko John stood up and said that it looks like we're not going to achieve consensus, so maybe we ought to let the matter stand for now while everybody thinks about these things.

So then someone said turn to page 201 and we stood up and sang:

> Faith of our fathers, living still
> In spite of dungeon, fire, and sword;
> O how our hearts beat high with joy
> Whene-er we hear that glorious word.
> Faith of our fathers, holy faith.
> We will be true to thee till death!

Then, with straight faces, Deacon Dan and everybody else sang the second verse about our fathers chained in prisons dark, were still in heart and conscience free, and how sweet would be their children's fate, if they, like them, could die for thee.

Oh, wow, something's wrong here, something doesn't quite add up.

About four o'clock Michael glanced toward the house and saw someone wearing a backpack turn into the driveway. Half an hour later, the same person, minus the backpack, was walking through the wheat stubble toward the plowed ground. He looked vaguely familiar. Michael studied the man as he drove toward the middle of the field. Suddenly he recognized him. It was Gimli! Seeing Gimli in this setting was about as mind boggling as if a visitor from outer space had suddenly made an appearance.

Michael smiled, remembering John Vandervoort rejecting his Dutch Reformed background, discovering Eastern religion, and proclaiming himself a Buddhist. Then discovering J. R. R. Tolkien and, identifying with Tolkien's dwarf, renaming himself Gimli.

Gimli stood now in the wheat stubble beside the plowed ground grinning at Michael as the huge machine approached.

Michael stopped the tractor, opened the door of the cab, and leaped to the ground. He and Gimli embraced, clapping each other on the back as they danced in a circle.

"Hey, man, it's great to see you!" Michael shouted above the sound of the tractor. "How did you know where to find me?"

"They gave me your home address at the Records Office. I called there and your mother told me where you were. I looked it up on a map and realized it's practically right on the road from Kalamazoo to Taos, where I'm headed, so I thought I'd stop off for a couple of days if it's cool with you and your aunt and uncle."

"Hey, that's great. The whole family will be glad to have you. Let's get out of this heat. Come on up and ride around with me. We can talk while we plow."

Gimli, seated beside Michael on the wide seat, watched with fascination as the big machine, hurried down the furrow trailing a wide strip of freshly plowed black soil. "Hey, it's cool in here. An air-conditioned tractor! Wow, man! That blows my mind!"

"Yeah, how about that?" Michael said, "I think the next step will be an unmanned tractor run by a computer. By the way, you didn't hitchhike out here, did you?"

"All the way, man, all the way."

"I'll bet a freak like you got plenty of hassle from the men hired to protect honest citizens from degenerate hippies and other undesirables."

"Twice in each state except Iowa. There they got interested in me three times. The last time, they gave me a ride to the Missouri border and suggested I take a different route on the way back."

"Did they get curious about what was in your backpack?"

"That seemed to be the main idea. They just knew it had to be full of the killer weed, the assassin of youth they always looked disappointed when they couldn't find anything even remotely illegal."

"Yeah, out here in Middle America, the home of the Silent Majority, folks take a dim view of flower children and dope."

"You know, I was getting bad vibes all the way out here, but here in Prairie Ridge people didn't look at me like they hated me the way they did everywhere else."

"I guess that's because Mennonites have always been out of step with the rest of society, so they tend to be more tolerant of other weirdos. Speaking of Prairie Ridge," Michael said, "did you have any trouble finding the farm from there?"

"I went to the post office and asked a guy there how to get to the Schrag farm. He looks at me kinda funny and whips out a telephone book, opens it, and lays it out in front of me and says, 'Which one?' I couldn't believe it! A whole page of Schrags! So I explain to the guy who I'm looking for. He points to your Uncle Andy's name. That's really neat the way the telephone book tells where everyone lives—so many miles this way, so many miles and a fraction that way. It's like pinpointing a spot on a checkerboard."

"Yeah, well, I guess we do live on a big checkerboard here." Michael said. "You know, when I was a kid, I thought the whole world was divided up into neat, square chunks of land like this."

"You mentioned Mennonites. I remember you told me once you were a Mennonite."

"We're all Mennonites around here. We're right in the middle of Mennonite country."

"Wow, man, this blows my mind! You know, I always knew Mennonites lived in bunches, so I figured, if you were a Mennonite, there'd be lots more of them around here, but I kept looking for horses and buggies, but all I saw were cars and pickup trucks and great big tractors. Lots of Buicks and Oldsmobiles, but no buggies. What gives?"

Michael laughed. "Yeah, that's the stereotype image most people have of the Mennonites. The horse-and-buggy Mennonites, or the Amish faction, is a very small part of the total Mennonite community, but because they're so visible, they are

170

the only ones people see and naturally suppose all Mennonites live that way. Out here the Mennonite farmers are all into agri-business."

"Wow! Horseless Mennonites into agri-business! That's heavy, man!"

Michael was silent for a moment. Then, as if he had just thought of it, he said, "Hey, if you want to see horses, my gran'dad will be more than happy to show you his."

"Yeah, I'd like to see them. Where does he live?"

"Right here," Michael pointed to the big Schrag farmhouse. "See that one-story addition on the side? That's where grandpa and grandma live."

"Far out, man! That's beautiful! A three-generation family in one house. Hey, that's the way it's supposed to be. With a setup like this, how come your dad and mom moved to Michigan?"

"That's my mom and stepdad. My dad was killed in the war out in the Pacific before I was born."

"I thought Mennonites didn't go in for war and crap like that."

"They don't usually. I don't really know what happened. Somehow he got sucked into it and was killed right after he got out there. Mom told me he never even knew she was pregnant."

"Wow, that's heavy, man."

Gimli continued to question Michael about his family, about the Mennonites, and about the farm. Suddenly he noticed the earphones hanging from the tape deck.

"Hey, man—wow—music! Fantastic!"

Michael grinned, pushed in a tape and handed Gimli the earphones.

Plugged in, Gimli closed his eyes and smiled, his body swaying to the music.

The sun sank through the osage orange hedge and half an hour later Michael power-levered the plow out of the ground and raced toward the house.

15

Michael and his Uncle Andy had agreed to take turns with the new tractor, so the next morning Michael took the old tractor to the west eighty. Andy, on the new tractor, began to plow on the south quarter where Michael had left off the day before.

The sun, bursting through distant hedge rows, climbed into the sky, drying the dew on the wheat stubble in the great square fields. The old red tractor roared its way north for half a mile, turned and roared back. Michael, his ears plugged against the deafening noise, was alone with his thoughts. He turned in the seat and watched the soil rise, crumble, and turn over under the plow, and thought that, in spite of all the discomfort of the old tractor, there was something to be said for not being encapsuled and insulated in an air-conditioned cab while he plowed the land. Contact with the soil is more immediate and, somehow, more personal. Of course it isn't like the old days when the plowman sat right on top of the plow being pulled through the fields by a team of horses.

Michael smiled, remembering Grandpa Jonas on his plow inviting a small boy to climb up and sit in his lap to go with him to the other end of the long field and back again. The little boy feels the man's strong arms on either side of him. He sees the strong hands holding the leather reins. The pungent smell of sweaty horses, of leather and wheat straw and wild roses mixes together and is all around them. The leather harnesses strain and creak, the trace chains jangle, the horses swish their great feet through the stiff wheat stubble, and when he listens closely, he can hear the soil as it turns over, crushing and burying the stubble and the scattered clumps of wild roses under it to become part of the soil out of which new wheat and little patches of wild roses will grow again. Meadowlarks sing and gentle Jonas says a word of encouragement now and then to the plodding horses, looks around at the land, at the sky, and at the soil turning over under him, and talks to the boy about the land and the things that grow on it.

To plow with Jonas is to learn that the earth is holy and the tilling of the soil is a holy vocation. The desacralization of the land, of nature, was, for him, a foreign, unthinkable concept. *And the Lord God took the man, and put him into the garden of Eden to dress it and to keep it.*

From the vantage point of his almost twenty-two years, Michael realized, in retrospect, that his grandfather had probably been more aware of his responsibility as a male role model for his grandson than most fathers are for their sons. It was obvious also that Jonas thought of himself as a stand-in for Menno and, by speaking to Michael almost every day about his father, he had brought Menno out of the shadows and had made of him a very real and living person.

There was some confusion, however, for Michael. Among his earliest recollections were stories of two men who had died violent deaths for the sake of others. They had died and yet, somehow, they were still around and were very much concerned with how people behaved toward one another. One of the men was called Jesus. His picture was on the wall in the living room. He had long hair and a beard and smiled and looked sad at the same time. The other man was called Menno. His picture was in a cardboard frame on the piano. He didn't have a beard. He was smiling too, but at the same time, looked serious. Up in heaven the two men must have known each other because their ideas of how Michael was supposed to think and act were much the same.

Another name for Jesus was Christ, and the Sunday school

173

teacher said that people who knew Christ were called Christians. Michael grinned, remembering that he had naturally assumed that people who knew Menno were Mennonites, and anyone who knew both were both Mennonites and Christians.

It had taken him a long time to sort it all out. After several courses in psychology, he had begun to think that maybe he still didn't have it all sorted out.

Having a father who was also a Christ figure was kind of tough sometimes. Other kids could brag about their fathers' exploits and prowess, but for him to do so would have been to bring his father down to the level of mere, everyday man and to confuse the sacred with the profane.

About nine-thirty, the sun, shining through the unshaded window, began to pry at Gimli's eyelids. He became aware of birds singing loudly in the trees outside the open window. Tractors droned in the fields. He groped at the side table and found his wire-rimmed granny glasses. Putting them on, he reached for his colorfully patched, faded jeans. He pulled them on, zipped them up, and retied the piece of clothesline cord he used for a belt. Next he slipped the embroidered, oriental shirt over his head, letting it hang loosely about his hips. Fumbling in his backpack, he found a comb and ran it through his long hair. He gathered it together and tied a leather shoestring around it, making a ponytail that hung halfway down his back. He ran the comb through his heavy beard. Next he looped a long string of beads around his neck, slipped his bare feet into his sandals, and was ready to go downstairs.

As he came down the stairs he could hear Michael's Aunt Sarah singing in the kitchen. Her back was turned toward the dining room door so she didn't see him standing in the doorway watching her. She put the finishing touches on the four loaves of bread dough evenly spaced on a large flat pan. Giving each loaf a final pat, she opened the oven and slid the pan in. She turned the dial to "warm" so that the yeast would activate the dough. As she worked she sang:

174

> Bringing in the sheaves,
> Bringing in the sheaves,
> We shall come rejoicing,
> Bringing in the sheaves.

She turned and saw Gimli smiling at her from the doorway. "Good morning," she said, smiling back at him. "You're just in time. I was about to have a cup of coffee. Now I'll pour two. Would you like some toast?"

"Oh wow. Sure. Thanks. Hey, that's great. I heard you singing. It was beautiful."

Pleased, Sarah turned back to the stove. Gimli went to the bathroom just off the kitchen. He could hear Sarah singing again as she worked.

> Sowing in the morning, sowing seeds of kindness,
> Sowing in the noontide and the dewy eve;
> Waiting for the harvest and the time of reaping,
> We shall come rejoicing, bringing in the sheaves.

Back in the big kitchen again, Gimli saw two cups of steaming coffee and a glass of orange juice on the chrome and formica table.

"Sit down," Sarah called out. "The toast is almost ready."

"Beautiful, beautiful," Gimli murmured as he sat down.

The toast popped up and Sarah buttered it, all the while humming "Bringing in the sheaves." She put the toast on a plate and set it in front of Gimli. "Oh yes," she said, "cream and sugar." She brought them, along with a jar of plum preserves, and sat down across from him. "Everyone was so tired last night we didn't get a chance to talk. Tell me about yourself."

His mouth full of toast, Gimli shrugged. He swallowed and said modestly, "There isn't much to tell."

"You know I told Andy last night you look just like I imagine my great-grandfather looked when he was your age. Of course I only knew him when he was old, but he had a big beard like yours, only when I knew him it was white. He was about your

175

size. In fact, people called him Kleine Sep, which is the German version of Little Joe. He even wore little round glasses like yours. When I was a little girl, he used to set me on his lap and tell me stories about his childhood in Russia."

Sarah spent her waking hours happily and enthusiastically talking. When she had no one to talk to, she sang. Having been reminded of her great-grandfather and his stories, she proceeded to tell Gimli the history of the Swiss Mennonites who migrated to Russia where they lived for almost a century before coming to the United States in 1874. Her story was embellished with many family legends. His occasional "Wow!" or "Far out!" or "Beautiful!" was all the reinforcement she needed.

When they had both finished their second cup of coffee, Sarah, who had always taken for granted separate work roles for men and women, was both amazed and pleased to see Gimli pick up his tableware as well as her cup, take them to the sink, wash them carefully and place them on the drying rack.

Finished, he told her how good the breakfast was, how great it was talking with her, and that he would like to go out and explore the farm. He went out through the screen enclosed back porch and stood for a moment squinting into the bright sunlight, looking around at the widely spaced farm buildings. Through the screen doors behind him he could hear Sarah singing:

O for a thousand tongues to sing
My great Redeemer's praise,
The glories of my God and King,
The triumphs of His grace.

Several hundred yards north of the house Gimli saw a large, arch-roofed, aluminum colored steel Quonset building. The building was obviously used for storing and repairing farm machinery. The doors on both ends were open and he could see the outline of a huge machine. He learned later it was a self-propelled combine used to harvest grain. He heard activity in the building and wandered over to investigate.

The noise coming from inside the building stopped just before he got there. Gimli stood in the high, wide doorway and saw David and Peter bent over a large sheet of paper they had unfolded and spread over the hood of a battered Volkswagen Beetle. The little car was set on four big blocks of osage orange wood. The wheels, dangling from the suspension system, just cleared the concrete floor.

The boys were dressed alike in faded jeans and grease-stained T-shirts with large peace symbols on the back. Their heads were covered with colorful caps with long bills. One was yellow and green, with the legend "John Deere," along with a stylized leaping deer on a patch above the bill. The other was yellow and white with "De Kalb" and an ear of yellow corn on the patch. The boys were so engrossed in studying the sheet before them they didn't notice Gimli.

"Here, here, and here," David said, jabbing the paper with his index finger.

"And here." Peter pointed to another location on the diagram they were studying.

David looked at it closely. "Yeah, right."

Gimli, grinning at them, raised his hand. "Hi."

"Hi," they answered together.

Peter went to the workbench and picked up a closed-end wrench and fitted a socket to a ratchet. He slipped on a pair of plastic safety glasses. One tool in each hand, he lay down on a scoot board. His head and shoulders disappeared under the Volkswagen.

David wheeled a cart with a pair of cylindrical tanks out to the middle of the floor. He unwound the long hoses looped around the handles of the two-wheeled cart, removed a brass nozzle from the fittings at the end of the hoses, and substituted another. From a small table made of angle iron and boiler plate, he picked up a pair of heavy welders' goggles, turned his cap around so that the bill covered his neck, and slipped the goggles on his head. As he turned two valve wheels on the brass fittings, there was a loud hissing. Directing the escaping gas away from him, he reached behind him and picked up a strange looking wire-spring device from the steel table. He held it about a foot from the end of the brass nozzle and squeezed the spring together. A spark ignited the gas, and a geyser of flame shot out. He laid the igniting tool back on the table and pulled his goggles down over his eyes. He adjusted the valves by turning the little wheels on the side of the brass fittings. The flame subsided into a thin, blue, six-inch cylinder of concentrated heat.

At the rear of the Volkswagen David lay down on another scoot board and pushed himself under.

Gimli examined the paper spread over the hood. At the top was a picture of a Volkswagen and at the bottom a dune buggy. The rest of the paper was covered with diagrams and paragraphs of instructions. "Wow, this boggles the mind!" he said to himself. "When I was their age I needed help changing a tire on my bicycle!"

As the boys talked to each other above the sound of the cutting torch, Gimli walked from the building shaking his head. "So this is what Mennonite farm kids do for their kicks! Wow!"

Outside in the bright, hot sun again, he could hear the roar of the big green tractor across the road. He heard another tractor west of the barn and, nearsightedly peering in the direction of the sound, saw the outline of it moving through the field Michael waved to him but got no response. He remembered Gimli's poor eyesight.

Gimli opened a small door near the corner of the big red barn. He stood for a moment inside waiting for his eyes to adjust to the dim interior. The ground floor of the barn protected from the sun's heat by an overhead mow of hay was relatively cool. The sweet smell of fresh alfalfa hay mingled with the odor of horses and horse manure. Horse sounds came from somewhere near the middle of the long row of stalls. Hay was being chomped and pushed around in mangers. A horse blew sharply through vibrating nostrils. Gimli stared in the general direction of the sounds and began to discern the rumps of two huge horses protruding from behind the partitions between the stalls. As he stared, a man walked toward him from behind the horses. He had white hair and, as he came closer, Gimli could see he had clear blue eyes.

"Good morning. You must be Michael's friend Gimli. I'm Jonas."

"Hi, Jonas," Gimli held out his hand. Jonas clasped it. The two men sized each other up. "Hey, man, Michael told me about you. He said you were beautiful people—in a fantastic head-space. He was right. You give off good vibes."

Jonas didn't quite know what to make of this young man and his strange way of talking, but he thought he was going to like him. "Would you like to see my horses?" Jonas gestured, indicating the great dapple-gray Percherons.

"Sure." Their size made Gimli a little uneasy.

"This is Dick. The other one is Duke." Jonas patted the huge gelding on the rump, his hand higher than his head. "Stroke his nose," Jonas said, "he likes that."

Gimli timidly approached the animal's head. Dick looked around at him and blew through his nose. Gimli jumped back, then gamely but cautiously extended his hand toward the horse's face. Dick met him halfway, nuzzling his hand. "Oh wow! Hey, his nose is like velvet! Oh, man, this is far out! Beautiful!" He continued stroking Dick's face with one hand, running the other over the dappled, silken neck and powerful shoulders.

"They look just like a team I worked with many years ago, so when I bought them I named them after that other team," Jonas explained.

"I've never been up close to horses like these before. Man, they're beautiful! Fantastic." Gimli's myopic eyes shone behind his thick-lensed, wire-rimmed glasses. "Hey, man, could I drive them? I'd really like that!"

Pleased, Jonas said, "Sure, but let's wait till toward evening when it's not so hot. Would you like to see the rest of the farm?

179

The other animals?"

"Yeah, sure. Great!" Gimli gave the big horse a final pat and followed Jonas out of the barn.

As the two men walked slowly toward the chicken house, Jonas said, "Andy and I farmed the whole place together for a long time, but a few years ago Anna and I decided it was time to slow down. We didn't want to move to town so we built on to the house so we could have our own little place. We turned the farm over to Andy and Sarah to run, but we kept twenty acres for ourselves." He pointed to four small, individually fenced fields. Several cattle and sheep were grazing in one of them.

"We have pasture, hay, oats, and corn. Every year we switch the crops around in the fields. It's better for the land that way. The alfalfa, though, lasts for about seven years, so we don't change that every year. With these fields and the garden over there," he pointed, "we grow 'most all the food for the whole family. Anna likes to spin and weave and knit, and that's what the sheep are for."

"Oh wow, man. That's really far out! Fantastic! Beautiful! You know I'm on my way to New Mexico to see if I can live in a commune where a bunch of people got together to try to live off the land. I don't know anything about how to live off the land, but I sure want to learn. Would you let me stay here for a few days and work for you so I could learn something about farming?" Gimli peered anxiously at Jonas. He looked like a little boy trying to hide behind thick granny glasses and a huge beard.

Jonas laughed. "Sure. Let's go see if Anna has the coffeepot on."

"Oh wow, man, you're beautiful!"

16

It was October. Michael, sitting in the Student Union, was reading a letter from his grandmother Anna. She wrote that Gimli had left for New Mexico that morning. He had, for a time, seriously considered staying in Kansas permanently, believing he had found what he was looking for among the Holdeman Mennonites north of town. His first encounter with them occurred when he had seen Henry Koehn on the street in town. He went up to him and asked him why he wore a beard. Henry had looked at him in surprise and told him he wore a beard to show that he was different from the people of the world. He then asked Gimli why he wore a beard, and Gimli, his eyes twinkling behind his thick granny glasses, told him he wore a beard to show that he was different from the people of the world. Then, to Henry's surprise and embarrassment, Gimli hugged him and told him he was beautiful. Henry was intrigued with the strange young man and, after a long conversation, invited him to church.

Gimli was fascinated with the "plain people" lifestyle of the Holdemans and with the beautiful simplicity of their church services. After several conversations with some of their preachers, however, he realized that he was not prepared to make the kind of commitment they would demand of him, and decided to go on to New Mexico.

The Student Union began to fill up as students, on a break between classes, converged from all over campus. This was the

181

social center for the university during the day and the students tended to separate themselves into groups with like interests. The "long-hairs" sat together in one corner, and the black students had the space next to them. Members of the more exclusive fraternities and sororities congregated in the opposite corner of the huge room. The more inclusive fraternities had their section in still another corner. Those students who didn't identify with any particular social group took up the remaining space.

Michael finished reading the letter and put it back in the envelope. A freshman with acne and a scruffy beard sat facing him across the square table. "Letter from home?" he asked.

"From my grandma," Michael smiled.

"What a drag. Old people are a drag."

"Not Grandma. She's beautiful. A really together person."

"That I'd hafta see. An old chick who's got it together. I've never seen one."

Tom, who Michael knew as a religion major, put his tray with a hamburger, Coke, and french fries on the table, pulled out the chair on Michael's left, and sat down. He hitched his chair closer. "My grandma's a real cool old lady, too. My old man, though, is a cretin. The only thing he ever says to me is, 'Get a haircut.' I try to talk to him. He looks at me and says, 'Get a haircut.'"

Tom's Afro-style blond hair formed a great golden halo around his head. He looked around the table. "As you all probably know, I have a thing about hair." He reached up and, with his palm, brushed the ends of his electric hair a foot from his scalp. "Hairs are living chains of cells that grow out of your skin. According to a certain rabbi from Nazareth, the hairs on your head are all numbered. The length of said hairs are usually a matter of personal choice. Medical science has yet to discover any correlation between length of hair and intelligence, morality, virility, cancer, or anything else. I really dig this phenomenon called hair. I don't care if it's curly, fuzzy, shaggy, ratty, matty, shining, gleaming, streaming, knotted, twisted, beaded, braided, powdered, flowered, bangled, tangled, or spangled."

"You made your point," Michael laughed. "Anyone who would memorize that list from the 'Hair' album has got to have a thing about hair!" Michael pointed to the hamburger Tom had started to eat. "That bronco any good?" he asked.

"Foolish question. Assembly-line techniques throughout its fabrication process insure that it tastes exactly the same as those made yesterday, the day before, tomorrow, and so on and so on."

"I think I'm hungry enough to eat one." Michael stood up and walked over to the cafeteria line. He ordered a bronco and leaned against the railing watching while it was quickly put together. Every hamburger dispensary seemed to have its own name for them. Each time Michael ordered one here he had to remind himself that they were named for the university football team, and the name had, one hoped, nothing to do with the source of the ground meat in them.

When he came back with his burger and a Coke, someone had taken his chair. He took a chair at another table. All three students at the table were reading while they nibbled and sipped. As Michael sat down all three glanced at him and said "Hi" and continued to read. He liked this relaxed way everyone in The Ghetto seemed to have. You could talk to the people around you or you didn't have to. What was the expression? "Hang loose." His grandparents would say "*gemütlich.*" Everyone here was "hanging loose," not "up tight" the way a lot of other people seemed to be. They didn't play the little social games the fraternity and sorority people were always into.

His table companions were Dave, Sue, and Jill. He didn't know their last names. Michael looked around at the other tables and realized he knew the first names of almost everyone there, but very few last names. No one seemed to bother with family names.

Dave looked up. "Hey, you gotta hear this. This is the Parris

183

Island U.S. Marine Corps yearbook." He held it up so the others could see the cover.

MY RIFLE: This is my rifle. There are many like it but this is mine. My rifle is my best friend. It is my life. I must master it as I master my life.

My rifle, without me is useless, without my rifle I am useless.

I must fire my rifle true. I must shoot straighter than my enemy who is trying to kill me. I must shoot him before he shoots me.

My rifle and myself know that what counts in this war is not the rounds we fire, the noise of our burst, nor the smoke we make. We know that it is the hits that count.

My rifle is human, even as I, because it is my life. Thus, I will learn it as a brother. I will learn its weakness, its strength, its parts, its accessories, its sights, and its barrel. I will keep my rifle clean and ready, even as I am clean and ready. We will become part of each other.

Before God I swear this creed. My rifle and myself are the defenders of my country. We are the masters of our enemy. We are the saviors of my life.

So be it, until victory is America's and there is no enemy but Peace!

"Wow! That's mind-boggling! Can you imagine being in a head-space like that? It sounds like the marine's love for his gun is almost sexual." Dave shook his head in amazement.

"Sure it is," Sue said. "How about the Beatles' number 'Happiness Is a Warm Gun?' "

"Did any of you ever read a poem by Henry Reed called 'Naming of Parts?' " Jill asked. "It's about a soldier cleaning his gun and naming each part as he cleans it. It's sexual from start to finish. Read it sometime. It'll blow your mind."

"I guess I have mixed feelings about guns," Sue said. "I don't like them, but we have to be realistic. I have to come down against gun control legislation. If there would be strict gun control in this country the blacks and leftists wouldn't be able to get them, but all the flaming Birchers and suburban reactionaries would still be armed to the teeth. I think the Constitution guarantees the right to bear arms in order to counterpose an armed populace to the armed state. Take the guns away from the cops and then you can take them away from the people. The cops aren't about to let their guns be taken away, so they shouldn't be taken away from the people either."

"I hate guns," Jill said. "I wish no one had them. When you talk about this group or that group being better armed than the others, you're talking as if they were playing some sort of chess game where you move gun pieces around to better advantage. In real life you don't draw a card that says 'dead,' you feel real bullets ripping into your body and breaking your bones and making holes for your blood to run out into the gutter. I don't want that to happen to anybody including cops. There has to be a better way and we had better find one. If we get guns we're just like they are, and if we're like them, we don't have the right or even a reason to fight them."

"Hey, you've really thought about this, haven't you?" Dave asked.

"Yes, I think there are too many people going around talking violent revolution who think it's nothing more than a fun game."

"I don't think it's a fun game," Sue said defensively.

"Oh, I didn't mean you. I know where your head's at and I know it's not just a game for you." Turning to Michael, Jill asked, "How about you, Michael? Where's your head in all this? You never say anything. You just sit and listen."

Michael grinned, "My granddad always says you learn more when you're listening than when you're talking. As far as where my head's at, I guess I always took pacifism for granted. My people are Mennonites and we've been pacifists for over four-hundred years. I guess it's never been an issue I've had to think much about. I was served pacifism along with my pablum."

"Wow! that's far out," Dave said. "I'm taking this course in the Reformation and I found out the Mennonites are really the Anabaptists of the sixteenth century. They were so radical you wouldn't believe it!" he explained to Sue and Jill. "They got together and told the establishment 'Screw you!' and when it came to war, they said, 'Hell no, we won't go!' Oh wow! they were beautiful people. You know," he continued excitedly, "they're still doing it. They live in separate communities and take care of their farms and tell the rest of the world to go screw itself."

"Well, it isn't quite like that," Michael protested.

"Where is this utopia you come from?" Sue asked.

"Kansas," Michael answered shortly, not sure if he was about to be put down.

"And I suppose when you're all done here you're going to say 'Screw you, world,' and go back to Camelot, or the Garden of Eden, or whatever, plant your turnips, or whatever it is they grow in Kansas, close the door behind you, and live happily ever after, while the rest of us are stuck here in the hurting, bleeding world?"

Michael could see she wasn't joking. "I guess I still have a lot of thinking to do," he said.

Sue looked at the clock. "Hey, I've got a class in Sangren. Gotta run."

Michael had a class too, but in the other direction. He was glad he didn't have to continue the conversation. His class was in the religion department. His graduate school adviser in the history department had approved of his choice of a class in religion, so he would get credit for it toward his MA in history.

Now that he had his bachelor's degree, he no longer had a student deferment from the draft and was, from day to day, expecting a notice from the draft board to report for his physical. He hoped they would at least give him time to complete the term.

The religion department didn't have its own space, so classes were scattered all over the campus wherever empty classrooms were available. "The Religious Factor in Social and Cultural

Change" met in a classroom in the field house. The gymnasium smell always reminded Michael that it was jock territory.

Otto Spengler was a popular professor. His classes were sought after, not only by religion majors, but political activists among the students competed for space in his classes. He was militantly Hegelian, and was often called a Marxist, but insisted he was a "Hegelian Existentialist," and a "Religious Humanist."

Otto, as his students called him, was a big man who liked to eat. He conducted class sitting in his chair with his hands clasped over his ample stomach. While his body appeared to be in complete repose, his large, round face, punctuated by piercing blue eyes, and haloed by Albert Einstein hair, was a study in animation. It was never his intent to lecture to his classes, but it always seemed to turn out that way. He started the class period with remarks designed to stimulate class discussion, but invariably got carried away with his subject and the students sat spellbound for the entire period, listening to a spontaneous outpouring of ideas and commentary on man, the sociopolitical animal.

He always looked startled when the buzzer in the corridor sounded at the end of the hour. Looking at the class apologetically, he would say, "Well! So! Next time, more class discussion!"

Opportunity for dialogue, however, came after the formal class period. The room wasn't needed again for twenty minutes, so the students who didn't have another class to go to stayed on to engage in lively discussions, with Spengler acting as referee.

While the students who had other classes to attend filed out of the room, Spengler gathered the books and papers on his desk, stuffing them into his fat briefcase, all the while answering students' questions in clipped German accents. At the start of each class period he removed books and papers from his briefcase and ritually laid them out in a neat pattern on his desk. They were completely ignored until, at the end of the period, he carefully gathered them up and returned them to the briefcase.

The class today followed the usual ritual, and he pried the last of the books into the briefcase as the last student to leave the room closed the door. He looked up then at the eight or nine students who had stayed behind. Pretending to be surprised to see them there, he said, "Well! So! You got nothing better to do? You want to sit around and talk, what? What is it you say—shoot the bull? Okay, we shoot the bull. You, Fritz," he looked at a black-bearded, intense young man, "you are a leader of men, yes? You want to be an agent for social change. You want to know how can you bring down the corrupt system that robs the poor and powerless, the wretched of the earth, and makes war on them so that it can reward the rich and powerful, yes?"

Fritz laughed. "How about doing it in stages? Right now we're into getting the genocidal maniacs in Washington to stop the killing in Vietnam. Do you think the march on the Pentagon this weekend will do any good?"

A student at the back of the room, whom Michael knew as Pete, said quickly, "That's a heck of a question coming from the president of the local chapter of SDS. I thought SDS was organizing the whole thing. Don't you have any confidence in what your own people are doing?" Pete asked reproachfully, baiting Fritz, hoping to get him excited and defensive.

"Yeah, sure," Fritz said. "That was just a rhetorical question I threw out to get some feedback. Sure I believe it'll do some good. When half a million people surround the Pentagon and yell like hell, somebody has to listen."

"Dream on," Pete said. "In the first place, half a million is a totally unrealistic figure, but, aside from that, how many votes do hippies have, and how many multinational corporations do they control?"

"You sound like you're about to give me that old song-and-dance about the only way to bring about change is by working within the system," Fritz said.

188

"I think there's something to be said for working within the system. Maybe it does bring about change more slowly, but it makes more sense than these sophomoric demonstrations by bunches of middle-class kids pretending to be *lumpen prole-tariat*,° marching around yelling slogans."

Fritz, ignoring the slur, slapped his forehead. "Here we go again! 'Work within the system!' Liberal crapola! God save us from liberals! Liberals have been 'working from within' for the last thirty-five years, and where has it got us? We can't wait around any more. The problem with liberals is that they have their priorities messed up. Their first commitment is to respectability. Social justice comes second. When it comes right down to it, the only difference between a liberal and a right-wing Bircher is that the liberal feels a little guilty that his af-fluence was bought with the blood and sweat of the poor.

"The liberal believes that politics is the art of compromise, so when he gets into politics, the first thing he does is com-promise. That's a fancy word for selling out. Maybe he feels a little guilty at first, but he soon learns to live with the guilt. It's the liberals that are in charge right now!" he said excitedly. "Old Hubert the Hump, McNamara, Rusk, Johnson—they're all liberals. Back in the thirties, Johnson was F. D. R.'s golden boy from Texas. Hey!" he looked around the room, "did you see that picture in the 'New Left Notes' of old Hubert yuking it up with General Ky? The old New Deal liberals started out to 'work within' the system to reform it and now they're burning babies in Vietnam."

"Hey," someone said, "old Fritzy's on his SDS soapbox again."

Pete grinned. He had Fritz going again.

Michael decided to get into it. "At the risk of appearing to defend the system, if you do away with the existing political structures, what are you going to put in their place? Wouldn't the absence of structure mean chaos?"

°In Marxist parlance, "Ragged working-class people."

189

"What we're saying," Fritz explained, "is that we don't need the authoritarian, paternalistic, manipulative system we have now. People should have the right to participate in making the decisions that effect their lives. We should be free from manipulation and coercion. We believe we shouldn't continually have to choose between alternatives established by someone else. We're not into setting up blueprints for a social and political structure. What we want to do is bring down the evil system we have now, and then let the people, without manipulation or coercion, organize a cooperative society that will allow universal participation. We believe that people are capable of understanding their problems and are able to participate in their solution. We don't need a 'Big Brother' to watch over us."

Fritz noticed several students grinning at him. He raised his hands in a gesture of surrender. "Okay, okay, I'm pontificating again. Actually, the reason I brought up the march on the Pentagon this weekend is to slip in a commercial. We've chartered two buses and we want to fill them. Spread the word. Okay?"

Students began coming into the room for the next class.

Spengler stood up. "Fritz," he said, "you tell them in Washington, Otto Spengler says 'stop the war!' All right?"

Fritz raised his fist in salute. "All right," he said.

Out in the hall, Spengler carried his heavy briefcase lopsidedly. He looked at Michael. "Michael Schrag," he gave it the German pronunciation, "future agent of social change!"

Michael smiled. Spengler wanted all his students to be agents of social change.

"Tell me," he said, his eyes twinkling, "for a man whose ancestors, with their radical, revolutionary ideas almost stood Christendom on its ear four hundred years ago, how does it feel, now that again revolution is in the air all around us? Are you as radical as your Anabaptist ancestors?"

Michael, taken aback, was about to stammer a reply.

"Ya, ya, I know. Very quickly those revolutionaries became

die Stillen im Land, but maybe now it's time to speak up again? No?"

Another student asked Spengler a question, and Michael walked on down the hall and out of the building.

As he walked up the hill and past the Student Center he noticed the leaves on the stately oaks around the president's house were showing their fall colors. He looked back across the valley and saw patches of crimson in the sugar maples on the old campus and the State Hospital grounds.

In the parking lot behind Sangren Hall, he got into his Mustang and drove home. Home was a three-bedroom apartment in a new complex west of the campus. His roommates, Sam and Beejay, with whom he shared housekeeping chores and rent payments, weren't there when he let himself in.

That night in bed Michael lay thinking of the implications of Spengler's reference to his Anabaptist ancestors. How had he put it? "Very quickly they became *die Stillen im Land.*" All his life Michael had heard about the early Anabaptists—Grebel, Manz, Blaurock, Sattler, and Menno—but they had always been mixed up with his image of hook-and-eye Mennonite farmers. He grinned as he remembered his childhood mental picture of Conrad Grebel taking time off from his plowing to go debate with Zwingli.

That wasn't the way it was at all! Those guys were well educated, urban, radical revolutionaries, and they stormed the very citadels of power with ideas that would háve swept away centuries of institutionalized corruption and evil and brought in a new order of peace and enlightenment. The second generation continued the struggle and were martyred along with their parents. It was about the third generation that fled to the boondocks, put the revolution on 'hold,' opted out of the political process, and declared themselves "the quiet in the land." The world wasn't ready for their kind of idealism, so they withdrew from the world, established disciplined, agrarian communities, and practiced their ideals among themselves.

As time went on separation from the world and the political

process became institutionalized to the point that most of them willingly placed themselves under the protection and authority of autocratic rulers in exchange for promises to be left alone to do their own thing. Even in this century, thousands of Mennonites left democratic Canada to live in the "green hell" of the Paraguayan Chaco under military dictators, so that they didn't have to participate in the political process and engage in political dialogue with the "people of the world." This can't be what Grebel and Manz and Menno had in mind.

Michael had seen a book in the church library called *The Recovery of the Anabaptist Vision*. He hadn't read the book, but now he wondered if a recovery of the vision of his Anabaptist forebears wouldn't involve storming the citadels of power once again with the message that there *can* be peace and goodwill among men, and that the ideals of the Sermon on the Mount *can* be made to replace the corrupt and bloody systems now in place. As Spengler said, "Maybe now it's time to speak up again, no?"

The next morning, over orange juice, milk, and granola, Michael said to his roommates, "How would you guys like to go to Washington this weekend?"

"You mean the march on the Pentagon?" Sam asked.

Michael nodded.

"I'd sure like to go and help stop the war machine in its tracks," Beejay said, "but I haven't got enough bread for a bus ticket."

"Got enough to kick in a little for gas for the Mustang?" Michael asked.

Beejay looked at Sam, eyebrows raised.

Sam shrugged. "Sure. Why not?"

"You got yourself a coupla passengers," Beejay said.

17

Michael woke up one eyelid at a time. Mellow light filtered through russet, gold, and green leaves. Birds sang and chirped in the trees. He closed his eyes and drifted back. He was in his bed on the farm in Kansas. It was morning. The birds were singing in the ash tree outside his window. He woke with a start and sat up. This is definitely not Kansas, he thought, but it's nice to know Kansas is only a dream away. As he unzipped his sleeping bag he stared at the Washington Monument. It soared into the early morning sky, the point of its pyramid piercing the brilliant blue canopy arched over the city. West of the monument patches of gray fog hung over the Potomac.

He crawled out of the orange-lined, green sleeping bag, stood up, and stretched his sleep stiffened muscles. The sun, not yet visible, was shining on the Capitol dome about a mile and a quarter to the east. Traffic noises were increasing on the White House side of the Mall. The city was coming awake. Squatting, he rolled up his sleeping bag, tying it into a neat bundle. He walked a few steps to the Mustang parked at the curb, opened the trunk, tossed the bag in, and gently closed the trunk lid. He didn't want to wake Beejay and Sam, still asleep in their sleeping bags on the grass beside the car.

Soon after they had arrived the night before, they had located a portable washroom on the opposite side of the mall north and east of the Washington Monument. Michael now headed in that direction, winding his way between hundreds of occupied sleeping bags. The grass, away from the trees, was wet with dew. As he approached the long, metal, boxcar-like portable latrine, the rim of the rising sun moved slowly up the left side of the Capitol dome.

Inside, Michael hurried. The smell of toilet chemicals was overpowering. As he slipped out the door, he was sure that he would always associate this chemical toilet smell with the city of Washington.

He walked back toward the car parked on the curving street south of the Mall. All over the Mall and under the trees on either side, a youthful Coxey's army was emerging from cocoon sleeping bags and from under blankets. This was the day of the march on the Pentagon, a modern-day storming of the Bastille. Would the fortress hold or would it crumble before the power of the people?

Back at the car Beejay and Sam were rolling up their sleeping bags. Neither was very communicative until after a trip to the latrine. The three young men then drank milk from their thermos jugs and shared a bag of granola.

Their hunger satisfied, they locked the doors of the Mustang and started to walk slowly around the huge mound of earth forming the base of the great monolith that dominated the landscape and skyline.

More buses were arriving every few minutes, disgorging passengers and driving on. The event was taking on a carnival atmosphere. Michael thought of his annual visits to the state fair in Hutchinson and smiled to himself. The patrons of the fair were never as colorful as this!

Beejay, Sam, and Michael, dressed in bluejeans and blue denim jackets, realized they hadn't dressed for the costume ball the march on the Pentagon was turning out to be. The soldiers of this citizens' army would have none of the drab uniforms of conventional militarists. When it came to a choice of uniforms, each marched to the sound of a different drummer. Here were the legions of Sgt. Pepper's band. There were Park Avenue doormen and Arab shieks. Here and there one saw Daniel

Boone, Jim Bowie, Kit Carson, or Wyatt Earp with his contemporaries at the OK Corral. A blue-clad Union officer stood beside a gray-garbed, red-sashed Confederate. There were Indians in war paint and Martians in green space suits, Batman and Robin, the Three Musketeers, and Paladin with his gun, ready to travel. An unhorsed knight clanked about in heavy armor among moon-men and witches. There were Jordanian shepherds, Indian gurus, Roman senators, and French legionnaires, but the most prevalent costume was the tie-dyed T-shirt, sandals, and threadbare jeans, faded, colorfully patched, and re-patched, many of them displaying an American flag sewn upside down on the seat, the ultimate symbol of defiance. Thus was the New Left Army of the Shining Republic arrayed for battle.

Along the north side of the long Reflecting Pool, about a dozen young people had shed their clothing and were happily cavorting in the water, splashing one another. They were not so much exhibitionists as children of Adam and Eve, recreating a pristine world. The Children's Crusade was about to begin.

Michael and his companions threaded their way through the milling crowd, past singing troubadours, chanting gurus, and philosophers engaged in earnest dialogue.

At the bottom of the steps of the Lincoln Memorial a speakers' platform had been hastily assembled. Young technicians were setting up microphones and testing them. The three young men walked around the platform and climbed the steps of the Memorial. At the top of the steps they were awed by the twenty-foot high statue of the Great Emancipator sitting in his chair, facing the Washington Monument and the Capitol. They turned to see what the great brooding Lincoln was eternally looking at.

"Wow!" Sam said, "The Capitol must be over a mile away."

Michael appeared to be calculating. "It's two miles."

"I'll take your word for it," Sam laughed. "Every time I've checked an odometer against your calculations, you were right on. I don't know how you do it."

"It's easy for him," Beejay said. "He figures distances in relation to the length or width of his Kansas wheat fields."

"You could grow a lot of wheat in this long field between here and the Capitol," Sam speculated.

"That would be a poor management decision," Michael said, pretending he had given it a lot of thought.

"You're the farmer," Sam said, pretending to yield to his superior judgment. "What are we going to plant here after the revolution?"

"Corn is the obvious crop. After all, there is already a silo in the middle of the field."

"Don't encourage him," Beejay said to Sam. "He's going to have us talking like cornball, hick farmers just like him."

People came and went, staring at the statue and reading the second inaugural address carved on the wall to Lincoln's left and the Gettysburg address on his right. A young woman walked slowly by. A year-old baby rode in a pouch strapped to her back. Across the baby's back was the inscription, "Babies are not for burning."

Loudspeakers squawked. A trumpet blared. The rally was starting. An almost solid mass of moving bodies filled the Mall from the Lincoln Memorial to the Washington Monument and beyond. Signs and banners were everywhere. Most bore slogans, but many spelled out the names of organizations. There were Students for a Democratic Society, American Friends Service Committee, W.E.B. DuBois Clubs, Catholic Peace Fellowship, Jewish Peace Fellowship, National Lawyers' Guild, National Conference for a New Politics, Veterans Against the War in Vietnam, Southern Christian Leadership Conference, The Resistance. Many signs simply had large letters printed on them such as SDS, SNCC, or SANE, assuming that everyone knew what organization the letters represented.

Red and blue Viet Cong flags mingled with signs affirming that "Che Quevara Lives." Several posters said "Dump Johnson." One read "Where Is Oswald When We Need Him?" A favorite was "Make Love, Not War!"

As Michael studied the crowd he was aware that, while young people predominated, middle-aged, middle-class professional people were also well represented.

Entry to the police-guarded, roped-in area between the speakers' stand and the steps of the Memorial was controlled by young men wearing arm bands. It was filling up with speakers, reporters, and TV cameramen. The excitement of an-event-about-to-occur permeated the crowd. Slogans were shouted. A group began screaming, "Hell no! We won't go!" Each time it was repeated more joined in until it was a mighty roar. When this ran down they began: "Hey! Hey! L.B.J., how many kids did you kill today?"

A group on the White House side of the Reflecting Pool danced and sang Israeli folk songs. On the other side people locked arms and sang "We Shall Overcome."

The speeches began. Midway through the first one, there was a commotion on the platform. A man was yelling. Several of the men on the platform wrestled him to the floor and the police carried him away kicking and screaming. Someone at a microphone said something about a Nazi.

After an hour the speeches began to be repetitive. The crowd became restless. Someone shouted, "We can listen to speeches anytime. We came here to march on the Pentagon. What are we waiting for?"

After yet another hour of speeches the march appeared to be getting under way. Conflicting orders boomed over loud-speakers. No one seemed to know quite what to do. Assaulting the Pentagon with this vast citizens' army gathered on the banks of the Potomac was not as simple and straightforward as it first appeared.

Michael and his friends followed the colonnade to the back, or Arlington Bridge side of the Memorial, climbed down to the retaining wall, swung themselves over, and dropped to the grass below. Cameramen waited in and around a convertible parked on the bridge about a hundred yards from the east end. The young men called Mobilization Monitors, distinguished by their armbands, shouted at the crowd through their loud-speakers, herding the marchers toward the approach to the bridge. Michael remembered a TV program he used to watch. "Head 'em up, an' move 'em out!" the trail boss had shouted while cattle-driving music played in the background.

A half dozen or more helicopters hovered and swooped overhead, chopping and battering the air. TV cameras poked from several. Two hundred or more marchers were now on the thirty-yard-wide bridge, and were halted by the young men with armbands and portable loudspeakers. "Dress up that line there, dress it up!" they shouted. "Come on, cooperate!"

The mass of humanity surrounding the Lincoln Memorial was pushing and surging toward the bottleneck at the bridge entrance. Michael found himself pushed against the base of a huge bronze equestrian statue on the south side of the bridge entrance. "Valor" it was named; an enormous horse and a great muscular man with his muscular spouse. A great pile of muscles cast in bronze and, according to the legend on the base, given to the people of the United States by the people of Italy. The matching statuary on the north side of the bridge included a child. The mass of people between prevented Michael from reading the lettering on its base.

The crowd continued to press toward the bridge and the armband people tried desperately to form an orderly march. Michael, pressed against the stonework at the bridge entrance, stared out over the river, fighting claustrophobia. He wondered why they didn't let those already on the bridge start walking across. The sides of the bridge would "trim up the line."

Someone must have eventually thought of this, and the march began again. It was more of a shuffle than a march as the crowd followed the backward-walking camera people.

Halfway across the bridge Beejay and Sam, who had been separated from Michael, maneuvered themselves into positions on either side of him.

"Hey, Farmer," Sam said, "imagine this is a wheat field instead of a river, and tell us how wide it is."

"It's half again as wide as a half-mile-long eighty-acre field, so it's three eighths of a mile wide."

"Now we know." Beejay grinned.

All three began munching peanuts and raisins from the bags they had put in their jacket pockets.

The packed bodies pushed from the rear. Those at the front of the mass kept pace with the camera crews and refused to be pushed into a faster walk. Michael fought to maintain his position next to the stone parapet where he could control his claustrophobia by looking out over the water. The shouting of the marchers and the incessant chopping of the helicopters was deafening.

The packed mass of humanity finally began to extrude from the bridge. In spite of the frantic efforts of the monitors, the crowd fanned widely over the grassy traffic circle west of the stone-eagle-guarded end of the bridge. The marchers were funneled over a short bridge spanning the boundary channel and, on the Virginia side, turned left toward the Pentagon.

The sweating, armbanded monitors shouted and screamed into their megaphones, trying in vain to confine the marchers to the narrow macadam road. The road here was parallel to the boundary channel on the left and a heavily traveled highway on the right. Several hundred yards of open grassland extended from the highway to the narrow boundary channel. The marchers, pouring from the bridge, spread out over the grass in spite of the best efforts of the monitors to confine them to the road.

Michael looked up at the roaring, chopping helicopters and wondered what this mass of humanity looked like from up there. He thought it probably looked like a single biological entity, a huge, dragonlike monster whose shape constantly changed as it squeezed through bridges and spread out over open land. The head of the dragon was the tight little group of publicity hungry, speechmaking notables who, arms locked together, closely followed the TV cameras which, carrot-like, dangled enticingly just beyond their reach.

The monitors, despairing in their efforts to keep the marchers on the road, confined themselves to preventing the flanks from overtaking and enveloping the head. Michael walked slowly on the grass between the tarmac road and the boundary channel.

The head of the dragonlike body of marchers disappeared into an arched underpass that looked like a crypt. The body pulled itself tightly together and followed into the narrow defile. A young black man stood on the stone parapet directly above the apex of the crypt-like arch fifteen feet above the marchers. He held up a placard that read: "No Vietnamese ever called me a nigger." The marchers cheered him as they passed beneath.

On the other side of the arched underpass the narrow road followed closely the curve of the shallow boundary channel. To the right of the road a grassy field sloped upward away from the river channel. The marchers spread out into the field, but were forced back to the narrow road again by a high barbed-wire topped, steel-mesh fence. The fence followed the road for several hundred yards before making a right-angle turn away from the road. When the marchers passed the fence corner they found themselves in the paved, thirty-acre parking lot called the North Parking Area of the Pentagon.

A four-lane highway separated the lot from the Pentagon. Access to the huge, five-sided building was across bridges spanning the highway. Michael, Sam, and Beejay stared at the pale yellow structure. Its pentagonal shape was visible only from the air. They could see only two of the five sides.

"It looks like an oversized Sears and Roebuck warehouse," Beejay said. "What do you call that kind of architecture?"

"I think it's called 'Twentieth-Century Ugly,' " Sam said, grinning.

They heard music coming from the side of the parking lot nearest the Pentagon. A group of musicians in bright costumes was playing on a flatbed truck. The group called the Fugs had been scheduled and, as the parking lot began to fill, the group began its entertainment. The musicians' colorful costumes included orange, yellow, and rose capes.

Abbie Hoffman, a war protest leader, had requested the General Services Administration to issue a permit for twelve hundred people to form a ring around the Pentagon, exorcise it, and raise it three hundred feet into the air. As it hovered in the air, he said, it would turn orange and vibrate until all evil emissions fled. The General Services Administration had, tongue in cheek, consented to let an attempt be made to raise the building—but only ten feet. They refused, however, to allow the encirclement.

As Michael and his friends approached the truck, the Fugs began their exorcism rite. Cymbals clanged, an Indian triangle was repeatedly struck, finger bells jangled, and a mournful trumpet wailed, providing an eerie musical background for a solemn incantation by a member of the Fugs:

> In the name of the holy acts of hearing, seeing, smelling, touching, groping, and loving, we call upon the powers of the cosmos to protect our ceremonies from the powers of evil and darkness in the name of Zeus, in the name of Anubis, god of the dead, in the name of all those killed because they do not comprehend, in the name of the lives of the soldiers in Vietnam who were killed because of bad karma, in the name of sea-born Aphrodite, in the name of Earth Mother, in the name of Dionysus, Zagreus, Jesus, Yahweh, the unnamable, Zoroastra, Hermes, in the name of the Beak of Sok, in the name of scarab, in the name of the Tyrone Power Pound Cake Society in the Sky, in the name of Rah, in the name of the vital, flowing universe, we call upon the Great Spirit to raise the Pentagon from its destiny, cast out the evil within it, and preserve it for the glory of God made manifest in man.

The trumpet, cymbals, triangles, and bells sustained a thunderous outpouring of air-shattering sound as the musicians chanted loudly, "Out demons, out! Back to darkness ye servants of Satan! Out demons, out! Out demons, out!" The amplifiers were turned higher, the tempo increased, the trumpet blared, the cymbals crashed, and the triangles and bells jangled frantically. The crowd joined the musicians. "Out demons, out! Out demons, out!" Over and over the crowd screamed as one voice, "Out demons, out!"

Beejay yelled into Michael's ear, "How many of these people do you think are taking this seriously?"

Michael yelled back, "I don't know, but it looks and sounds like a lot of people are putting everything they've got into it."

Attention was torn from the exorcism rite when a group of several hundred men, marching in a tightly packed wedge, moved quickly onto a ramp leading to a bridge to the Pentagon. Those at the point of the wedge carried Vietcong flags. Bushes prevented Michael from seeing the encounter with the military people guarding the bridge. In a few minutes the men, terror on their faces, rushed back to the parking lot.

Michael was pushed back to the high wire fence at the edge of the lot. Through the noise of the musical instruments on the truck, the shouting, chanting crowd, and the chopping, hovering helicopters, he heard excited talk of clubbing by the military police and U.S. marshals. He saw blood on the faces of several of the young men.

When the Fugs packed away their equipment, having failed to levitate the Pentagon, loudspeakers began blaring from a speakers' stand several hundred yards away. There were to be more speeches. Most of the marchers were not in a mood for speeches and milled about, listening to rumors and passing them on.

Michael found himself at the south edge of the parking lot where a line of military police were thinly spaced behind a rope barrier stretched about a foot from the ground. Some ten yards behind them was another line of MPs, and behind them, clusters of U.S. marshals in white helmets and dark-blue suits.

A few feet to Michael's left a young woman in jeans, a head-band, and sandals was staring closely at a young MP. The man's stoic face was partially hidden by mirror sunglasses.

"Hey, wow!" the young woman exclaimed, "This guy's got tombstones in his eyes!"

202

Michael stepped behind her and looked into the sunglasses. They were reflecting twin images of the Washington Monument across the river.

Michael pushed his way back into the crowd while ambulances wailed and rumors of vicious beatings and cracked heads swirled about him. Suddenly he was aware that he was being borne along by a wave of excited people pushing through a big hole in the fence which separated the parking lot from the highway. Caught up in the excitement, he was one with the surging mass that poured across the four-lane road and onto the mall at the north entrance of the Pentagon. The demonstrators were stopped short of the doors to the building by a solid mass of young soldiers backed by U.S. marshals.

The front line of soldiers stood impassively, rifles pointed at the demonstrators. The invaders milled about indecisively. Tension was relieved when some of the marchers began putting flowers into the barrels of soldier's rifles.

Fearful that a sudden charge by the military would result in many casualties, demonstration leaders, speaking through megaphones, urged the marchers to sit down.

Michael had been jostled into a position next to the front line of soldiers, so that when he sat down, he was inches from a pair of thick-soled military boots. He was very aware of the M14 rifle directly over his head.

The soldiers, under orders not to speak, stared silently over the heads of the demonstrators, their rifles in firing position. Some of the demonstrators began to heckle the soldiers while others pleaded with them to throw down their rifles and join them. "I am you, and you are me, and we are all together," they said. "Join us and help us fight our common enemy, the criminal warmongers in the Pentagon."

The marshals, wearing their blue suits, white helmets, and mirror sunglasses, paced back and forth behind the MPs, smacking their clubs against the palms of their hands, glaring malevolently at the demonstrators. Michael watched them and wondered at their hatred.

The marshals seemed to want action. Several times demonstrators, pressed against the first line of soldiers, accidently hit a soldier's shin or knee with an elbow while turning. This was an excuse for the marshals to reach through the MP lines, jerk the offenders through, beat them with their clubs, and drag them away.

Fresh troops from the interior of the Pentagon relieved those on the lines every half hour.

Some time after dark a young man burned his draft card. He held it high for the cheering crowd to see, and passed it along until it was used to ignite another card which in turn was passed on to ignite still another. Each time a card was set aflame the crowd roared its approval.

As the sequence of burning cards came nearer, Michael thought of his own card in his pocket. If he ceremonially burned it here as a symbol of his solidarity with these his brothers, protesting the evil of war, would he not be a hypocrite? As a Mennonite he had been given the privilege of alternate service where he would be spared the horrors of war. To burn his card now while his brothers and sisters cheered, would be a farce. They would cheer, not knowing of his special status. If he really wanted to make a statement, he should turn his card in to his draft board, tell them he was refusing to participate in any way with the draft, and then take the consequences.

The violence and the threat of violence surging around him reminded Michael of his father. Menno too had had special status as a Mennonite. But when he embraced the violence that caused his anger, his father must have realized that to continue to claim conscientious objector status would have been hypocritical. He had no choice then but to submit to the army, accepting its uniform, its weapons, and its institutionalized violence.

Michael wondered if his father had felt a sense of redemption when he interposed himself between the rifle and its victim.

As this was going through his mind he became aware of a commotion at his side. The young woman who had been sitting on his left had been pulled through the two lines of soldiers, and U.S. marshals were clubbing her. Blood began to stream down her face as she screamed in pain and terror. Without thinking, Michael flung himself between her and the vicious clubs. He felt the blinding crash of pain in the back of his head, and then nothing. The march on the Pentagon was over for him.

18

A week later Michael was back on campus. His experience at the Pentagon had left him with a wound on the back of his head that had required ten stitches. It was healing rapidly, but he still experienced headaches as the result of a severe concussion. The doctors at the hospital in Washington had assured him, however, that there was no permanent damage.

He was surprised at the attention he was getting. Apparently the only battle casualty among the marchers from Western, he was frequently recognized and pointed out all over campus. The student underground newspaper, *The Western Activist*, devoting an entire issue to the march on the Pentagon, had on its front page a clear, enlarged picture of him lying on the ground with two marshals clubbing him. He was identified in the caption, and his name was mentioned several times in the accompanying story. The entire university community seemed to believe he was a radical political activist. SDS members sought him out to share their ideas, believing his experience had made him a comrade-in-arms.

Through the remaining weeks of the fall term he was increasingly drawn into discussions about the student protest movement.

The editor of the officially recognized student newspaper *The Western Herald* asked him to write an article about his views on the war and the draft. His essay, articulating the immorality and futility of war, appeared in early December. The concluding statement was a call to refuse to obey the demands of the state to participate in immoral acts against the social order of the world community.

His call to civil disobedience was widely read. He came to be regarded as a leading campus radical. Students for a Democratic Society included his name in their list of core members which they sent to national headquarters.

The greater his involvement with the activists, however, the more uncomfortable he became. The people who were pulling him into their circle were all single-mindedly dedicated to what they called The Revolution. Sometimes he envied them their dedication. At other times he was appalled at their naiveté, castigating himself for his gullibility in being drawn into activity that, at best, was an exercise in futility.

Michael's last class in the fall term was on Wednesday, December 13. Early the next morning he pulled out of the parking lot behind the apartment building, and was on his way to Kansas.

He had decided to spend the holidays on the farm when he learned that his mother and stepfather were going to Kansas for Christmas. Roy could take only one week from his work, so he and Rachel were going to fly. Michael, however, had three weeks between terms, and had decided to drive out and see the country on the way.

The events of the past months had left him confused. Questions he thought had long ago been answered were again wide open. Things were moving too fast. There was too much pressure. He thought that if he could spend some time back in Prairie Ridge with his family and friends, he could put everything into perspective. He'd be able to get his head together.

Traffic was light as he headed west on Interstate 94. The wide highway was dry and the Mustang hummed along just under the seventy-mile-per-hour speed limit. The early morning sun was warm on his neck. He felt good. Time to relax—mellow out. Too uptight. Stay away from Marx and Marcuse.

Get into Alan Watts—*The Way of Zen. The Joyous Cosmology.* Learn to meditate. Chant a mantra—ooooooohmmm—ooooooohmmm. Riot clubs flash—draft cards burn—students yell. Shut them out! Concentrate! ooooooohmmm—no, don't concentrate, let go—let it be. Groove on what *IS*, not on what should, or ought to be.

Look around. Early winter landscape, the land resting, settling down to sleep. Smiling sun sending a weak message from far away over the tropic of capricorn—"Sleep well, Land of the North, I'll be back to wake you up next spring!"

A platoon of apple trees, having been marched with military precision to a strategic position on a hillside, stands guarding the house and barn at the foot of the hill.

Apple trees—.

> Now as I was young and easy under the apple boughs—
> Time let me hail and climb
> Golden in the heydays of his eyes,
> —I was prince of the apple towns

Dylan Thomas—*Fern Hill.* The story of my life.

> And as I was green and carefree, famous among the barns
> About the happy yard and singing as the farm was home,
>   In the sun that is young once only,
>   Time let me play and be
>   Golden in the mercy of his means.

Then comes the fruit of The Tree of the Knowledge of Good and Evil, and

> —the children green and golden
> Follow him out of grace,

Loss of innocence. You can't go home again. "So he drove out the man; and he placed at the east of the garden of Eden Cherubims, and a flaming sword which turned every way, to keep the way of the tree of life."

Gotta get out of this terror-of-history trip. Escape from history. Get into Zen. Forget clocks, calendars—time. Time is only an invention of man. Flow with the rhythm of my own being. Get in tune with the cosmos. Transcend. Get into Cosmic Consciousness—oooooohmmm.

Not easy, trying to get your head together. Too many ways to go. Too many possibilities. Start to go around in circles—faster and faster, tighter and tighter. Finally explode—or would you *im*plode?

—not with a bang but a whimper.

Sign ahead. "Expressway Ends One Mile."

Welcome to Indiana, Honorable What's His Name, Governor. A southbound, two-lane road connects to the Indiana Turnpike. Loop around, stop at the tollbooth. A smiling woman hands you a ticket. Smile back and take the westbound ramp that beckons travelers to Chicago.

Indiana Turnpike—Ohio, Pennsylvania—eight-hundred-mile-long corridor slashed through the land, paved over and fenced against intruders. Travel from New York to Chicago and back, and never discover America. Everything the traveler needs, provided at regularly spaced, look alike, plastic service centers. No need to cross the fence and fraternize with the natives. The planners are getting us ready for the Brave New World.

Back off, Michael. Stifle your paranoia. Thought you were going to stay away from this terror-of-history trip.

The heavy bank of cloud that had been looming in the west, now began to envelop the car. Traffic became heavier. He was in the industrial steel-mill area along Lake Michigan's south shoreline. Caught in the middle of what seemed an endless, double convoy of transport trucks, Michael was tense and apprehensive. The sun became a pale disc in the midmorning sky and finally disappeared altogether, obliterated by the thick smog that turned day into night. He kept glancing nervously into the rearview mirror at the lights of a truck only a few yards behind him. The taillights of the truck a few yards ahead of him were only visible because he kept squirting generous streams of windshield washing fluid on his fast-moving wiper blades. The tires on the truck ahead and on the truck keeping pace with him in the left lane were spewing black slush directly at him, completely covering the little Mustang. Hang in there. Somewhere on the other side of this the sun is shining.

Welcome to Illinois, Land of Lincoln. The sun was visible again. Traffic, still heavy, was thinning. Finally it was over. The sun shone. The pavement was dry, and most of the trucks had turned off to deliver their cargoes to the City of the Big Shoulders, the Nation's Freight Handler, and brawling Hog Butcher for the World.

The construction of superhighways in the Chicago area seemed to be going on constantly, so that every time Michael passed this way the roads were new and different. After several time-consuming detours, he crossed the Des Plains river and found Interstate 55. He sped along. He was getting away from America's foundry and was entering America's breadbasket. He could feel the tension drain away.

The large, green, overhead signs that spanned the road intermittently began announcing Joliet. He passed by the city and a few miles to the south the expressway ended and he was on old Route 66. He kept looking around him at the rich, level farmland of north-central Illinois. The corn and soybeans had been harvested, and most of the land was plowed for next spring's planting. The black clods of soil turned over by the plow were outlined and accented by white, powdery snow that had drifted and settled into the declivities between them. The large, square fields were mosaics of black and white. Scattered farmsteads and a few trees interrupted the straight-lined horizon. Here and there fields had been left unplowed and were covered with row upon row of tangled, V-shaped, dead cornstalks ravished by giant harvesting machines.

The level, black soil reminded Michael of Prairie Ridge, and he remembered that, according to a soil map in a physical geography textbook, it was the same kind of soil. Agronomists

say the soil, called loess, was wind-transported silt that had settled out from dust storms over many thousands of years. The
map showed a great mass of it, three feet to one hundred feet
thick, covering most of the corn belt on both sides of the
Mississippi and extending over half of Nebraska as well as
northern Kansas. There was a large island of it surrounding the
town of Prairie Ridge.

The Mustang's tires hummed over the pavement and
thumped rhythmically over the evenly spaced, tar-filled joints
between the slabs of concrete. A car with an Ontario license
plate passed. Canada. Toronto. Big. Clean. No slums—neat,
old brick row houses—ten coats of paint on the wood trim.
Ten-foot-square lawns. Tripping around from one ethnic
neighborhood to another is like a trip around the world.
Crowds on Yonge Street at midnight. Everyone feels safe. If
you dig cities, Toronto is the place to be. Rather live in the
country around Kitchener though. Wall-to-wall Mennonites.
Like home.

He was gradually creeping up on a big car ahead of him.
Half the cars on the road had bumper stickers advertising
either some tourist trap or, more often, the owner's political or
religious philosophy. This is a two-sticker car. Both stickers—
red, white, and blue. On the left, the word THIS, with a Christian cross beside it. On the right, NOT THIS, and a peace
symbol.

Pull around. Check them out. An American Gothic couple
stare at him sourly. Isn't it obvious you have to choose between
the two symbols? "We know who you are," their eyes said.
"You with the hair. You're one of them."

Thirty miles later a heavy-duty pickup truck pulled up
beside him. The driver, a large florid-faced man, his features
contorted with anger, was talking rapidly and emphatically. He
was alone in the truck and was looking at Michael, his anger
apparently directed at him. The truck began inching toward
the little Mustang. Michael moved over until he was forced
onto the shoulder. The truck made a final swipe at him, and

211

Michael braked to a stop. The angry driver sounded his horn and sped away. A large caliber hunting rifle hung in a rack over the rear window. His bumper sticker read, "America, love it or leave it!"

Long hair and beards mean you don't love America so, get out, Hippie!

Come on hands, stop shaking.

At Bloomington he took the business route through the middle of town and found an automatic car wash. Northwestern Indiana had left a thick coat of black slush on the Mustang that had dried to a mottled gray. He stayed in the car as it was pulled through the thrumming deluge of soapy water and whirling cylinders of flailing soft fiber. Outside again, the car wash attendants gave the little green car a few final swipes with their chamois and it glistened in the sun.

A little over an hour later he was approaching Springfield. He had stopped here once and visited Lincoln's tomb. Lincoln. The Lincoln Memorial. The march on the Pentagon. What was accomplished, other than getting a few heads cracked—including his own? Time would tell. Maybe the statement made there was heard, and would eventually have an effect. It was one of many ongoing demonstrations against the war. Water dripping on a stone, given enough time, will change the shape of the stone.

Getting back to Lincoln, the Great Emancipator. Sorry, Abe, but in spite of what we read in our grade school textbooks, the Emancipation Proclamation, rather than a manifestation of your altruism and concern for your enslaved black brothers, was an inspired afterthought born of the need to toss a sop to the noisy abolitionists, and the need to punish the rebels. You did it because it was politically expedient. The Northern liberals could, after that, see the fratricidal slaughter as a "just war," a "holy crusade," to which they could give their unreserved support. Smart move, Abe. Your black brothers appreciate it even if over a century later they're still not completely free of their chains.

Route 66 became a limited-access expressway around Springfield. A sign indicated the approaching exit led to highway 36. On an impulse, Michael turned. The route took him on a zigzag course through the city and out the west end. He had never taken route 36 before and felt like exploring new territory. West of the city the farms were smaller, there were more trees, and the land tended to be more rolling and scenic than along route 66 between Joliet and Springfield.

He crossed the Mississippi at Hannibal. Huckleberry Finn and Tom Sawyer lived here. Huckleberry Finn plied these waters in a raft, and somewhere in those bluffs on the Missouri side was a cave where Tom and Becky were trapped. Michael had been fascinated by Mark Twain's Mississippi when the only rivers he had seen were, during the summer, ankle-deep and narrow enough to jump across.

Back when the Civil War broke out, they tried to make a cavalry officer out of young Samuel Clemens. After two weeks he deserted and went out west to Nevada Territory. As an older man, Mark Twain had some caustic comments to make about war. Michael remembered reading a statement by him to the effect that man is the only animal that deals in the atrocity of war; that he is the only one who, for sordid wages, goes forth in cold blood to exterminate his own kind. "He has a motto for this," Twain wrote. " 'My country, right or wrong!' and any man who fails to shout it is called a traitor."

A few miles into Missouri, highway 24 branched off number 36 to the south. The map indicated it was a more direct route, so Michael turned. The next time the road widened into a small-town main street, he stopped to eat.

As he stepped from the car and walked toward the restaurant, the townspeople on the street stared at him. Inside, the place was full of customers. Conversations were loud and boisterous. As in every small-town eating place, when the door opened everyone turned to see who was joining them. Michael stepped through the door and the noisy room became silent. People stopped talking in mid-sentence, their mouths open.

213

Making his way toward an empty table in a far corner, he glanced nervously about at the silent staring faces, trying to determine whether they were hostile or friendly. He sat down, deciding they were only curious.

Conversation gradually resumed and people returned to their eating, glancing at him from time to time. Several young women with look-alike aprons were clustered around the kitchen door. They kept looking toward his table and seemed to be arguing among themselves. Finally, a middle-aged woman, probably the manager or owner, came to his table and took his order.

Michael looked at his fellow diners and tried to figure out why his entrance had caused such a reaction. When he noticed that all the men and boys had very short hair, and most had crew cuts, he smiled. He was probably the first "hippie" they had ever seen.

After eating, he paid his bill. The middle-aged woman took his money and, as she handed him his change, asked, "Are you a hippie?"

Michael gave her a friendly smile. "No, ma'am, I'm a Mennonite." He grinned as the woman walked to the back of the room to explain to the waitresses why he looked the way he did.

He drove only a few more miles through the rolling farmland when the sun settled into the western tree-covered hills and disappeared, leaving a rosy glow in the sky. The air turned frosty. The dark began to move in, reducing the world to a long, narrow, concrete slab outlined by shadowy forms that slid past the car. The first likely place to find a bed was in the town of Moberly at the junction of U.S. 24 and highway 63. The town advertised itself as being at an elevation of 858 feet and proud to be the boyhood home of General Omar Bradley.

The lights of the town were still ahead of him when he saw the faded sign, "Cabins, Reasonable Rates."

A flickering red neon arrow pointed to a row of small, peeling cabins beside a low, shabby house that looked like the cabins except that it was somewhat larger. A hundred-watt bulb on a post in front of the house illuminated the front door with the word "Office" stenciled over it. A sign on the door invited, "Come in."

Michael pushed the door open and stepped inside. An elderly couple were watching TV. The office was their living room. They stared at him suspiciously.

"I saw your sign," he said pleasantly. "I'd really appreciate a bed for the night."

"You by yourself?" the woman asked, squinting at him.

"Yes, ma'am."

She got up and opened a ledger on the table.

The man lost interest in him and returned to *Gilligan's Island.*

"Sign the book," the woman said. "And be sure you write down your license number." She held out her hand, palm up. "Six dollars. In advance."

He gave her the six dollars and wrote his name and license number in the ledger. She handed him a key with a large 2 stenciled on an attached card.

"Thank you," he smiled. "Good night."

She pulled a shawl over her shoulders and followed him to the car. She peered inside, then carefully studied the front license plate, her lips moving, "Better check it with what he wrote down in the book. Can't be too careful—him being a hippie and all."

Michael moved the Mustang to number two. There were no other cars. On the narrow, hard bed he went to sleep almost immediately. In the morning he woke up in the dark, splashed cold water on his face at the sink in the corner, brushed his teeth, pulled on his clothes and, bag in hand, stepped outside. The air was crisp and cold. Stars, scattered about the sky, were fading to make way for the sun climbing toward the horizon.

He started the Mustang, got out again, and scraped the frost from the windshield and windows. A big, blood-red neon sign across the road blinked its message to the world, "Ruby's Restaurant, Truckers Welcome, Open 24 Hours."

The square, flat-roofed, frame building sat well back from the road, allowing truckers to park their rigs while they ate. Gravel crunched as Michael drove into the parking lot. Engines idled in two waiting trucks. Gray-blue diesel smoke, rising from their shining, nickel-plated stacks, hung high above the trucks in the still, frosty air.

Inside, a tired, sharp-faced woman stood behind the counter watching him as he approached and sat on a stool. He smiled at her.

"Coffee?" she asked, not returning the smile.

"No, thanks. I'd like a cheese omelet, whole-wheat toast, and a glass of milk, please."

The woman disappeared through a swinging door behind the counter.

Two men, bacon-and-egg-stained plates on the table between them, sat smoking over cups of coffee. They stared at Michael. "How long you gonna be around here?" one of them asked.

"I'm on my way to Kansas," Michael answered pleasantly. "I'll hit the road again as soon as I've eaten."

"There's a barbershop in this town, two chairs, no waiting, opens at eight sharp. They could turn you into a clean-cut American in no time flat. Wouldn't cost much either. Fact is, if you ain't got the money, Ed and me, we'd be glad to pay to see you get cleaned up. Sort of our boy-scout-good-deed for the day."

Michael smiled at them, hoping this wouldn't turn into a bad scene. "Thanks for your generous offer. I might take you up on it if I wasn't in such a hurry to get back to my family on our farm in Kansas."

The reference to family and farm had the desired effect. The men lost interest and returned to their coffee and cigarettes and to talk of time schedules and speed traps.

When the woman brought his breakfast Michael ate quickly, paid, and left.

Highway 24 continued to wind through pleasant, rolling

country with well-kept farmsteads surrounded by fenced fields and pastures interspersed with woodlots. Cattle, standing on the sunny side of barns, stared at him as he drove past the farms.

He turned on the radio. The Morman Tabernacle Choir sang, "This land is your land, this land is my land, this land was made for you and me." He sang along with them. Beautiful! You can sing it and feel a surge of patriotic pride—not flag-waving chauvinism, but a patriotism that is love of the land. This land is my land! Nothing wrong with getting a little misty-eyed about spacious skies and amber waves of grain, and purple mountain majesties above the fruited plain. Just don't get carried away and buckle on Uncle Sam's terrible swift sword and go trampling out the vintage where the grapes of wrath are stored.

Love of the land unites people. Flag-waving divides and alienates. Interesting word—alienate. Alien—to not belong. The opposite of being alien is being native, indigenous, fulfilled, in harmony with your surroundings, at home. Your environment makes you welcome, and you gratefully repay it with respect, praise, loyalty, i.e., patriotism. The flag-waver, though, tells me I don't love America because I am unwilling to fight to preserve The American Way of Life which he always talks about in capital letters. He declares me an alien—out of harmony with my surroundings, unfulfilled, not at home, unwelcome.

A whole generation of Americans—alienated—separated from the culture. Paradoxically, their alienation is a tie that binds them together—The fraternity of the alienated coming together to create a counterculture. You could feel it there at the Pentagon. Brothers and sisters—solidarity forever—us against them.

How did it happen—this counterculture, a culture that is counter to, in opposition to, American culture?

Somewhere he had read an essay in which the writer offered a theory of what the alienation of youth was all about. He

217

wrote that American society had become so affluent that, for the first time, large numbers of young people were spared the necessity of entering the work force to survive, and instead, were enrolling in universities where they were able to reflect on and judge the society that spawned them. What they saw was a sick society that institutionalized selfishness, hypocrisy, greed, oppression, and war. Appalled and outraged, they rejected the culture and its system of values, and experimented with new ways of relating to the world and to one another. A counterculture. Aliens from the American way of life.

Paul McCartney came through the radio speakers. "I know you—you know me. One thing I can tell you, you got to be free. Come together—right now."

At Carrollton, 24 joined 65 and the highway, with both numbers on its identification signposts, headed south, crossing the Missouri river at Waverly. Separating here from 65, 24 headed west again. Traffic heavier. Independence coming up. Independence—starting point for the Oregon and Santa Fe trails. Home of Harry S. Truman—Give 'em Hell Harry, dropper of atom bombs. Independence becomes Kansas City ... flour mills, packinghouses, gin, and sin. Two thirds of the way through the city a sign welcomes travelers to Kansas, the Sunflower State.

U.S. 40 had joined 24 somewhere in the city and the double-duty highway, bridging the Kansas river just over the state line, continued west. Michael stayed on 40 when 24 veered north to jog its way west through a more northerly tier of counties.

West of Topeka the highway began to cut through the Flint Hills. Here is another of nature's creative works of art. A limestone plateau, fifty miles wide and a hundred and fifty miles long, stretching across the state, north to south. Great, sloping hills and ridges covered with virgin, blue-stem prairie grass. A world almost the way God made it. It is here the westward traveler first experiences the Great Plains. The sense of space, of vastness, is overwhelming. This land is my land, this land is your land, this land was made for you and me.

218

Between Manhattan and Junction City the highway followed the high rim on the south side of the valley where the Smoky Hill and Republican rivers converged to form the Kansas. On the north bank of the river, on the flat valley floor, and extending into the hills beyond, was Fort Riley. Camp Funston, Michael remembered hearing, was on the flatland near the river.

An exit sign indicated a town named Ogden. He could see the road crossing the valley to the little town across the river. He slowed and turned. Just over the bridge, he turned left.

Camp Funston. This is where Grandpa Jonas had his encounter with the military. He felt strange. This place actually existed. Shabby, small, and trashy, but tangible. He couldn't remember when he first heard of Camp Funston, but it had always been a legendary place for him, sharing mythic space with Mount Sinai, the Sea of Galilee, and the village of Kotosufka, where his great-grandparents were born.

The flatland between the river and the hills to the north was checkerboarded with gravel roads and chain link fences. Rusty, discarded military hardware lay in fence corners. Frame buildings, gray from weather and neglect, stood forlornly, shedding the last freckles of yellow paint still clinging to their walls. Boys in army fatigues, learning to be soldiers, stared at him. He turned west on the narrow road paralleling the railroad track, and drove past the first capitol of Kansas, now re-roofed and restored for tourists.

Get back on the highway. This valley is depressing.

U.S. 40 followed the valley of the Smoky Hill River, keeping to the low, grass-covered hills on the north. Abilene coming up. Abilene's claim to fame is that it was the terminus for the famous Chisholm Trail. Shipping point for Texas longhorns driven from the arid plains of Texas, fattened on Flint Hills bluestem grass, and loaded on cattle cars bound for Chicago and points east; after which the trailhands spent their hard earned money enjoying Abilene's night life.

That was nineteenth-century Abilene. The town's twentieth-century claim to fame came as a result of the local Brethren church losing one of its boys to West Point.

At Salina Michael turned south. As he approached Lindsborg the winter sun touched down on the hazy hills in the west. The setting sun outlined a square, fortress-like structure on the top of the highest hill overlooking the valley. Coronado Heights. His mother had taken him there once. Strange experience. It was a Sunday afternoon. He was about five. He and his mother were alone. They got out of the car and his mother led him by the hand to a big red rock. She sat on it and pulled him onto her lap and squeezed him so hard he could hardly breathe. He struggled. She let him go, and he went exploring around the top of the hill, turning over red and yellow stones, and climbing up and down the steps of the big stone building. He kept looking at his mother. She sat with her arms crossed in front of her, sort of hugging herself, and rocking back and forth, staring off into the smoky hills to the west. There was a funny look in her eyes. He couldn't tell if she was happy or sad. When the sun started to set she got up, smiled at him, took his hand, and went to the car. She sang to him on the way home. She never spoke to him of the incident. Later he wanted to ask her about it, but he knew he shouldn't. Something to do with his father. Something private. Sacred.

The lights of McPherson came on as the winter twilight turned to dark.

Paul Simon sang through the car's radio speakers.

Michigan seems like a dream to me now.
It took me four days
to hitchhike from Saginaw.
I've come to look for America.

Back to the land of the checkerboard farms.
This land is my land.
Home.
He drove up the long driveway. The porch light was on. He

had called from Kalamazoo before he left, so he was expected. As his headlights swung toward the house, Brownie exploded from under the porch and launched a noisy attack on the Mustang, determined to tear the tires from the wheels. Michael pulled up to the walk leading to the porch and got out of the car. Looking at the furiously barking, aggressive bundle of fur, muscle, and teeth, he laughed. "You're definitely not a Mennonite dog," he said.

At the sound of the familiar voice, Brownie dropped to his belly, groveling and whining. Michael reached down and rubbed the thick brown fur on his back. The dog jumped to his feet and danced around him, barking excitedly.

The door opened and Andy stood under the porch light. As Michael ran up the steps, Andy grabbed his hand and, at the same time, clapped him on the back. Laughing, he pulled Michael through the door to the waiting family. Clustered around the door, they interrupted each other in their eagerness to greet him. Jonas, Anna, and Sarah hugged him in turn, while David and Peter, smiling broadly, one on either side of him, shyly reached out, touching him on his shoulders.

Sarah hurried to the kitchen to prepare supper.

19

Except for Jonas and Anna, the family slept late the next morning. Jonas was at the barn at the usual time to take care of his animals. Milk from the family cow was cooling in the refrigerator when the rest of the family finally got up. Breakfast was a festive occasion with Sarah happily serving pancakes, eggs, and sausage.

After breakfast everyone gathered around the piano. Sarah played while Andy, Michael, David, and Peter formed a quartet and sang hymns in harmony. This was the family's favorite entertainment. Andy often spoke nostalgically of the men's quartet he had been a part of years ago. He had tried to get the men together again several times, but the others didn't share his enthusiasm.

"I think we're losing a great tradition," he complained. "When I was a kid, half the people in church were into quartets or some sort of choral group, besides the regular choir. Mennonites back then were known for their singing, but very few seem to be interested anymore."

"We still have the choir," Sarah said.

"Yeah," Andy shrugged, "but only half as big as it used to be."

In the afternoon David and Peter insisted Michael go with them for a drive in their dune buggy. Dressed warmly against the cold December wind, Michael drove the little vehicle for miles over the straight, level roads while his cousins extolled the virtues of their mechanical creation.

On a visit to Michigan the year before, they had seen a dune buggy driving along a beach on the Lake Michigan shore. The driver had stopped near them, and the two boys examined the vehicle closely. After a long conversation with the owner, they were determined to build one of their own.

"I wish we had sand dunes and beaches here," David said.

Michael looked around at the level, frozen fields of dormant winter wheat. "How about going to the sand hills on the other side of the Little Arkansas?" he suggested.

"Yeah, okay," David said. "It's not the same thing as the Lake Michigan dunes and beaches. But let's go check it out anyway."

Peter, sitting on his hands to warm them, made no comment.

Michael turned south at the next crossroads. Osage-orange hedges outlined many of the half-mile-square fields, their thorny branches etched against the cold, gray sky. About every half mile they passed a farmstead, a house surrounded by barns and granaries, still-life paintings frozen into the flat landscape.

Just before crossing the bridge over the small, tree-lined river, Michael remembered the old flour mill that had stood here beside the river when he was a child. It was gone now, and a patch of dry, winter-killed weeds covered the site.

Driving for an hour back and forth through the brown, grass-covered sand hills, Michael and his cousins saw that all the land was fenced and cross-fenced for cattle, and were reminded again that it bore little resemblance to the sand shaped by wind and water along Lake Michigan's shoreline.

The bone-chilling wind began to penetrate their heavy clothing, and they headed back to the farm through intermittent snow flurries. In a little while they were in the large, warm kitchen. Their heavy outer clothing removed, they sat around the kitchen table drinking hot cider spiced with cinnamon, and nibbled hard, spicy *Pfeffernusse* while Sarah brought Michael up to date on what had happened in the community since he had left in September.

That night the wind howled around the big square house. It died down about daylight, and Michael saw, when he got up, that only a little snow had fallen. The wind had kept the level, frozen fields swept clean. The drifted snow lay in long, ribbed ridges on the south side of buildings, fences, and hedgerows.

The drifts weren't deep enough to stop the cars. At the Sunday church service the building was full. Michael enjoyed the Advent sermon. The family had discussed the new preacher on the way to church. Michael learned that his name was Dan Martin, he was from Ohio, he had graduated from Oberlin before earning his degree from the Mennonite seminary, he was a little radical, and he was well liked.

After church Michael visited with his friends whom he had not seen since September. He missed several who had been drafted and were in alternate service.

The following Sunday was Christmas Eve. In addition to the Sunday morning church service, the family attended the traditional Christmas Eve program put on by the children. Michael sat with his mother and Roy. He had picked them up at the airport in Wichita the previous day.

Michael spent the week between Christmas and New Year enjoying his family, helping around the farm, and visiting again with friends and relatives.

On Wednesday he and Ruth Gering drove to Wichita. They wandered through an art gallery and a museum, then had dinner and went to a movie. The two usually spent some time together when Michael was in Kansas, but the relationship had never gone beyond a close friendship.

Ruth had a small, informal wine-and-cheese party at her house on Thursday evening. The dozen or more guests were all close friends of both Ruth and Michael. Two were seniors at the University of Kansas, and the rest were students at the Mennonite college in Newton.

The conversations were generally about social concerns, commitment to peace, and of student demonstrations against the war. The two university students, Jon Zerger and Sue

Krehbiel, spoke of graduate students who had gone to Canada to avoid the draft, and of a graduate student whom they both knew who had refused military induction and was sentenced to five years in Leavenworth.

"The war resisters," Jon said, "remind me of our ancestors in sixteenth-century Switzerland. Most of them fled the country, but some stayed and accepted prison or martyrdom."

"At least here, you guys have another alternative," Ruth said.

"Tell us about this guy that was sent to Leavenworth," Ken, a sociology major, said. "Did he try to get conscientious objector status?"

"No, he didn't try," Jon said.

"Why not, if he felt that strongly about it?"

"He believes that to accept alternate service is a cop-out. He says that if this war is going to be stopped, it will be when enough men like him lay their lives on the line and say 'no' to the warmongers. He would probably have qualified as a conscientious objector, but he said that to ask for it is to side-step the issue, and at the same time to acknowledge that his life belongs to the state."

"It seems to me," Ken said, "that while you're doing time in Leavenworth, your life surely belongs to the state."

"As my friend Mark put it," Jon said, " 'the state may seize my body, but they won't get my soul.' "

Ruth chose a square of cheddar from a plate of assorted cheese and began to nibble as she passed the plate along. "I don't think the war will be stopped by people making dramatic gestures."

"Hey, that isn't fair," Jon said. "When the peace churches got together and petitioned the government to allow us to do alternate service, I think it was a great thing, and I'm all for it, but I don't think we should accept it uncritically as our right, and then be critical of those who feel they have to deal with the problem another way. Each individual has to dig deep within himself and come up with answers that he can live with."

"I apologize," Ruth said. "What I said was pretty dumb. The self-sacrifice of a single individual for the redemption and liberation of the many should not be a new or surprising concept to people who profess to be Christians."

"You mean this guy thinks of himself as a Christ figure?" Ken asked.

"I'm sure such a thought never occurred to him," Jon said, "especially so, since he thinks of himself as a Buddhist."

"Did the FBI or the U.S. marshals come after him?" Michael asked.

"No. On the day he was supposed to report for induction, he turned himself in to the FBI instead," Jon said. "He wanted to spare them the trouble of looking for him."

"How long has he been in Leavenworth?" Michael asked, "and have you heard anything from him?"

"He's been there three months now," Jon answered. "I got a letter from him last week. I wish I'd brought it with me so you could all read it. The horror he's going through is unbelievable."

"Weren't a couple of Hutterites beaten to death by guards in Leavenworth back in World War One?" Ruth asked.

"Well, they died in Leavenworth, but they had just been transferred there from Alcatraz. It was the guards in Alcatraz that beat them. Mark says that most of the guards in Leavenworth have that quality of sadism which seems to be a prerequisite for the job but, while they know why he's there, and hate him for it, they haven't beat on him."

"How does he get along with the other prisoners?" Michael asked.

"Those men are prisoners of the U.S. government. You'd think they'd see him as someone who was there for defying the government, and would accept him as one of them, but most of them are very patriotic and despise him for being too cowardly to fight for his country. When he was there about a month he was badly beaten in the exercise yard. The guards took their time rescuing him. He was unconscious by the time they got to him. He spent a week in the prison infirmary and then two weeks in solitary confinement. A few days after he was back in his regular cell, a prisoner murdered a guard in the corridor just outside his cell. It must have been a grisly scene. The prisoner cut off the guard's head before the other guards could overcome him. It was a horrible thing for Mark to witness. He is not only in constant danger of being beaten or even killed, but he has to be forever on guard against rape."

"Rape?" Ruth asked, incredulous.

"In a violent society where there are no women, young men are in constant danger of rape," Jon replied. "It goes on all the time in prisons. Officials and guards know it but do little or nothing about it."

"This whole thing boggles the mind," Ruth said. "Everyone knows that prisons exist, that they are a fact of life, but hardly anyone knows what goes on there. I guess we don't know because we don't want to know."

"You seem to be telling us that spending up to five years being terrorized and brutalized is a viable alternative to government-allowed alternate service," Ken said. "That is," he added, "if you live that long."

"I'm only telling you what one person decided was an alternative," retorted Jon.

"Does he still think he made the right choice?" Michael asked.

"He didn't say," Jon said. "I wish I'd brought the letter so you could read it yourself. I was amazed at his compassion for others, and at his serenity. He sees the violence and brutality, not in terms of perpetrators and victims, but he sees everyone as victim. He seemed totally at peace, and his main concern is for the welfare of the brutalized people around him, both prisoners and guards, and for his own spiritual growth."

Ken turned to Michael who was sitting beside him. "When Uncle sends me greetings, I'll gladly volunteer for the bedpan brigade."

Michael looked at Jon. "When you graduate next spring, old

Hershey and his boys are going to be waiting for you. What are you going to do?"

"I don't know, but whatever I decide to do, it'll have to be a decision I can live with."

The group continued to discuss the philosophical and practical aspects of the various alternatives. Several vigorously defended their decision to accept alternate service.

Michael listened closely. He had said nothing of his involvement in the march on the Pentagon. At first he had wondered why he was reluctant to speak of it to his Kansas relatives. After thinking about it he realized he wasn't ready to tell them because they would understand it as a first step in a commitment to confrontation with the military that, once made, would have to be carried to its ultimate conclusion. Anything less would mean that he had only been playing a silly game.

He envied those of his friends who, without seeming to feel the need of self-examination, were comfortable in their acceptance of alternate service. Why couldn't it be that simple for him? The government had recognized him as a conscientious objector. Why couldn't he just accept it and go on from there? Was it because of his father? Did he so much want to be his father's son that he must also reject alternative service?

It was late when Michael drove home. The porch light had been left on for him. He switched it off and turned to lock the door behind him when he remembered the door didn't have a lock. He smiled. No one locks his door in Camelot.

Upstairs, he undressed slowly and crawled into bed. A half moon shone through the window, forming a square patch of light on the floor. Michael stared at the moonlit window, fragments of the evening's conversations going through his mind. Jon's friend had said that to accept alternate service is a cop-out; that the state could seize his body but they couldn't have his soul. The war will be stopped when enough people say "no." Ruth had said that the self-sacrifice of a single individual for the redemption and liberation of the many was a concept not exactly alien to Christian thinking—or something like that.

He drifted into sleep.

A distant rumbling became louder. The ground began to shake. A great cloud of dust was moving toward him from the east. Michael stared. A Sherman tank? It couldn't be. It was a machine larger than a forty-acre field. Wheels higher than two-story houses turned inside expressway-wide tracks that churned everything before them into dust, and left behind a wide trail of devastation. The huge machine had five sides and looked like it was made of pale-yellow stone. Olive-green men with bullet-shaped heads stared out of the double rows of windows on all five sides. The unspeakably foul smell of rotting corpses filled the air. Michael shuddered with revulsion.

Across the front of the advancing monster, letters, each ten feet high, proclaimed: "The United States of America War Machine." Just below the lettering a platform projected from the front of the machine. A man sat on the platform behind a desk covered with buttons. He controlled the machine by pushing these buttons. The man was large. He had long ears, and his gray hair, slicked down with hair-oil, was combed straight back from his forehead. From time to time he looked up from the buttons and said, "Mah fellow Americans, come let us reason together!" His voice had a curious twang.

Michael looked under the machine and saw wide, sinister looking, flexible tubes hanging from the monster's belly. They seemed alive as they swung this way and that, searching, probing. A tube reached out toward a young man. He disappeared. Michael stared, horrified. Another tube swung out and another young man was sucked into it, disappearing into the belly of the great machine.

Looking around him, Michael saw thousands of people in the path of the advancing monster. He was surprised and puzzled at the way most of them were reacting. Instead of looking at the machine with horror and revulsion, they seemed to regard it as a benign presence, or at worst, a necessary intrusion. Children continued to play. They seemed unaware that the machine even existed. Most of the middle-aged people stood around smiling. Many of them displayed huge lapel buttons that read, "America's Silent Majority, Member in good standing."

Somehow Michael knew that the probing tubes had been sensitized with a peculiar kind of radar that could detect certain letter-number combinations on cards in the pockets of the young men. When the radar found the right combination, the men were sucked into the machine. Most of those sucked in seemed programmed to accept it, and as they disappeared into the tubes, smiled and waved to their families and friends who stood watching and smiling, chests swelling with pride.

But some of the young men, seeing a suction tube pointing at them, ran. They always seemed to run in a northerly direction. When this happened, the parents with the big, round lapel-buttons on their chests broke their silence and cursed their sons as they ran, and then hung their heads in shame as neighbors looked at them with scorn.

As Michael looked on, several young men fashioned large, round peace symbols, and when the suction tubes reached for them, they clung to the symbols that were too large to go into the tubes. The tubes tugged at them for a few moments, then let go and passed them by.

Michael searched desperately for material to make a peace symbol. There was none. He ran to Jonas's pile of osage-orange fence posts, grabbed two and, with a length of barbed wire, tied them together in the form of a cross. The wire was longer than needed, and he used part of it to tie himself to the vertical post. His hands firmly clasping the horizontal post, he swung around, the crossed posts interposed between himself and the suction-tube.

With a roar the tube was upon him, pulling and straining. The barbed wire bit into his flesh and his muscles felt the strain as he clung to the crossed fence posts. The machine passed on and the suction tube left him to search and probe elsewhere, vacuuming more human bodies into the belly of the great beast.

Michael, lying on the ground, felt the weight of the crossed posts on top of him. He removed the barbed wire from his waist, pushed the posts aside, and stood up. The machine had moved on, and in its wake, men wearing blue suits, white helmets, and mirror sunglasses were gathering up the resisters. They put them in cages and stacked the cages on an olive-green, two-ton, flatbed truck. The men who reached for Michael were completely devoid of facial expression as they thrust him into his cage and stacked it with the others on the truck.

Workmen unloaded the cages and lined them up in neat rows inside a huge building with an aluminum-colored dome.

Michael looked through the vertical steel bars of his cage and suddenly they weren't vertical. They were horizontal, and were made of wood, not steel. He was a little boy peering between the boards of the pigpen. His grandfather and two of his uncles were beside him looking into the pen. Another uncle was on the other side of the fence, inside the pen. He had a knife. A big white pig lay on the ground thrashing convulsively. Blood gushed from the pig's throat in thick surges. The uncle's knife and his hands were covered with blood. The horizontal boards were vertical again and were steel bars. The white pig was not a pig at all, but a man in a strange kind of uniform. He was on the concrete floor, his arms and legs flailing and jerking spasmodically, his back arching and twisting. He made whistling, gurgling sounds, and blood gushed from his throat, pumping over the uncle's knife and his hands. No. The man with the knife was not an uncle. He was a wild-eyed stranger.

An eerie, whimpering cry began to build in the wild man's throat. He bent over the man on the floor and, with his knife, began to saw frantically at his throat. There were uniformed men standing bunched together about twenty feet from the wild man. Their faces were frozen in horror at what they saw, but now they started forward. The wild man, from deep in his throat, screamed at them and, dropping his knife, grasped the ears of the man on the floor and jerked. The head separated from the shoulders. The face was in repose, eyelids only half closed over the glazed eyes, the jaw was slack and the tongue protruded loosely between parted lips.

The wild man grasped the severed head by the hair and swung it in a wide arc like a baseball pitcher winding up. Blood splattered the uniformed men. They cringed, falling back. With a final despairing scream the wild man hurled his grisly ball at the uniformed men. It slipped from his grasp a second too soon and came crashing through the bars of Michael's cage and hit him in the chest.

He woke with a hoarse cry. By the time he understood he had been dreaming, he was sitting up gasping for air. In a moment he lay back down, sweating and trembling under his blankets.

The following Sunday was his last before returning to classes. As Michael sat in church waiting for the service to start, he wondered what Dan Martin was going to talk about. He had found his last two sermons interesting but, beyond certain presuppositions he seemed to make, his radicalism had not been apparent.

After the congregational singing, choral anthem, and the usual preliminaries, Martin began to speak. His opening statements presented a case for the radical nature of Christianity. He cited the revolutionary Jesus who, against the apparently irresistable force of history, stood for the *what ought to be*, rather than the *what is*. Discipleship or *Nachfolge*, as the Anabaptist forebears called it, is to stand with Christ against the demonic forces of evil, refuse compromise, and to remain faithful regardless of the consequences."

Michael listened intently as Martin continued. His sermon was a plea for the followers of Christ to take his revolutionary teachings seriously and to stop compromising with the forces of evil. He said that if the church would remember its true identity as the body of Christ, the prince of peace, and act accordingly, the leaders of our nation would begin to see that the teachings of Jesus of Nazareth pose as great a threat to the American military-industrial complex as it did to the Roman Empire.

"The church," he said, "has lost its prophetic voice. Just as Adolph Hitler could, in the name of the German people, systematically slaughter six million Jews while the church in Germany said nothing, the American government is today, in the name of the American people, committing vile atrocities in Southeast Asia with the support of what has been correctly called "Civil Religion" in America.

"Are we content to allow a smiling Lyndon Johnson number us with his 'Great Silent Majority,' or shall we unite our anguished protest into a great unified 'NO!'?

Martin summarized with: "To follow the radical path of Christianity is simply to be obedient to Christ. This is the path of liberation. To find freedom through obedience may sound paradoxical, but such obedience frees one from all slavery to human institutions and expectations. It is a radical liberation from the tyranny of possessions, of fear, and of death. It is the freedom to *be*.

"Obedience does not mean to choose the easy answer and then stop thinking. Rather, obedience rejects the easy answer of the status quo and requires one to think more deeply. Obedience means that decisions will not be made on the basis of avoiding suffering, but on the basis of what is right, even though it leads to a cross. Discipleship is costly."

That afternoon Michael spent several hours in his room lying on his bed, staring into space. About four-thirty he looked out of the window and saw Jonas on his way to the barn. He went downstairs, put on his heavy jacket and his barn boots, and followed him.

By the time he got to the barn, Jonas had started to feed the animals.

"Mind if I milk Spitzy?" Michael called out.

233

"I don't mind if Spitzy doesn't," Jonas laughed.

Michael picked up a milk pail and a stool and approached the wide-rumped, roan cow. He spoke to her in a soft voice and ran his hand over the thick winter hair on her back. Spitzy, so named because of her pointed teats, stopped chewing and swung her head around. Leafy alfalfa protruded from both sides of her mouth. She sniffed at Michael's arm. Her dim mind seemed to recall him and, relaxing, she turned back to munch the green, succulent hay.

Sitting beside her right flank, Michael placed the pail beneath her udder and tipped it slightly forward, holding it in place with pressure from his ankles and the calves of his legs. He blew on his fingers to warm them, and began to stroke her milk-stretched udder and still flaccid teats. The pointed teats filled with milk and, as Michael squeezed, the milk streamed into the metal pail in sharp, liquid-pinging spurts. As the level of milk in the pail rose, the sound subsided to a soft, bubbly, rhythmic shushing. He was reminded again that milking a cow is like riding a bicycle. Once you learn, you never forget.

The top of his head pressed softly into Spitzy's flank, Michael watched the rising foam in the pail as he made quick, darting holes in it with the pulsating streams of milk. Inhaling the warm, fragrant steam that rose from the pail, he listened to the sounds of cattle and sheep chewing hay, and of horses grunting and blowing as they chomped their oats, grinding it between their great teeth.

He breathed the barn smells and smiled to himself. For the moment he could dismiss the war, the draft, the Pentagon, U.S. marshals, and the SDS. He was at home.

After Jonas fed the animals he began cleaning the stalls and pens. Finished with the milking, Michael found a fork and helped him. When the manure that had accumulated overnight was added to the pile behind the barn, the two men each opened a bale of oat straw and scattered the dry bedding over the floors of the stalls and pens.

Spreading handfuls of the bright yellow straw in Spitzy's

stall, Michael asked Jonas, "If you had it to do over again, would you do the same as you did in 1917?"

Jonas, pushing straw around with his fork, was silent a moment, then said, "Things are a little different now than fifty years ago. They didn't have alternate service programs set up back then like they do now. There wasn't much of a choice then."

"The Hutterites back then believed they had a choice."

Jonas, his fork now still, looked at Michael. "Yes," he said.

"Do you believe we Mennonites have the moral right to the special status given us as conscientious objectors?" Michael asked.

Jonas sat down on a bale of straw. "Years are supposed to bring wisdom, and someone as old as I am should have answers. I guess I'm just not old enough yet."

Michael placed a bale of straw on the concrete floor and sat on it, facing Jonas.

Reflecting a moment, Jonas said, "Back when I was your age, and war broke out—The Great War, they called it then—everything was different. Our people were mostly still like they were in Russia. We didn't mix with others—only for business. Everybody still talked German. We stuck together. We were afraid. In some ways things were worse for us here than in Russia. It was only in the last years in Russia that they threatened us with military conscription. That's why our people left. We heard afterward that the government changed its mind and let Mennonites do alternate service, working in the forestry service. *Forsteidienst*, it was called.

"Here, in 1917 they marched us off to army camps and put uniforms on us. They didn't force us to become regular soldiers, but they kept talking to us about our duty to our country, and since our country was in the right, it was our duty as Christians to fight for the right. The officers would take us, one by one, into their offices and use all kinds of arguments to persuade us. A favorite was, 'If someone tried to rape your women and kill your children, wouldn't you defend them?'

Our Elders had told us they would put that kind of pressure on us and that we shouldn't argue, but say simply that, as Mennonites, we didn't believe in war and violence.

"We Mennonite men stuck together there in the army camps, and we got through it. At first it wasn't so hard for me because I didn't doubt that I was right. Right was right and wrong was wrong. It seemed pretty black-and-white to me.

"Then I learned to know some of the other men in the camp; men who were being trained for war. They were Christians too. They were shipped out, and later we heard that some of them were dead. They had died for what they believed in. Things weren't so simple anymore.

"And then we heard that two Hutterite men had been beaten to death in prison. They also died for what they believed."

Jonas and Michael sat silently for a moment, staring at the straw at their feet, each busy with his own thoughts.

"They sent us home then," Jonas went on. "The war that was fought to end all wars was over, but we only had time to get turned around when they were at it again.

"Our Menno—" Jonas's voice broke. "Our Menno believed that he shouldn't take part in war, that for him to be a soldier was wrong, but he stumbled and fell, and the great evil, the ugliness, pulled him in and he died." He wiped the tears from his cheeks with his sleeve. "We have the satisfaction though of knowing that he didn't kill, and that he died so that another man could live, so maybe there was some meaning to his dying. They put a uniform on him and made him carry a gun, but he was never a soldier."

"But he went through basic training," Michael protested. "They must have taught him—"

"No," Jonas said, "the last day he was at home he sat where you sit now and told me he resisted the training and had learned nothing of soldiering. He was at peace. He knew he would never again do violence to another person."

Jonas was again silent for a moment. "After that war there was Korea, and now Vietnam. The killing again—the butchery—women and children. The young people are right to protest. The killing must be stopped.

"You asked if we have the moral right to special status as conscientious objectors. I've thought a lot about that, and I keep going back and forth with it. Most of the time I say yes, but sometimes it bothers me. Sometimes I think that maybe now we shouldn't be silent anymore. We should join the college students and tell the government to stop the war, and try to get other people to see that what our government is doing is wrong."

"Grandpa," Michael said quietly, "I know now what I have to do."

"*Ach, Junge,*"° Jonas looked at Michael, his eyes brimming, "sometimes hard decisions have to be made when there is only you and God." He stood up and stepped toward Michael, laying his hand on his shoulder. "Michael," he said softly, pronouncing it the German way, three syllables, separated, and equally accented. It sounded like a benediction.

He gave Michael's shoulder a final squeeze and walked to the opposite side of the barn where he took a brush and began brushing Dick's glossy, dapple-gray coat. The great Percheron turned and nuzzled his arm.

Michael picked up the pail of milk and walked slowly to the house, not noticing the brutally cold wind, or the snow flurries that, swirling around him, were beginning to accumulate in little drifts on the leeward side of buildings and fences.

The day after he returned to Kalamazoo, Michael received his draft notice. He wrote the draft board a letter, stating the reasons why he could not participate in the draft. He enclosed his draft card and dropped the letter into the red, white, and blue mailbox on the corner.

°Oh, young one.

Translations

Page 31

An English version of this German hymn reads:

A mighty fortress is our God, a bulwark never failing;
Our helper He amid the flood of mortal ills prevailing;
For still our ancient foe doth seek to work us woe;
His craft and pow'r are great, and arm'd with cruel hate,
On earth is not his equal.

Page 157

A translation of this German hymn would read:

All men must die;
All flesh is as grass;
That which lives must decay,
and become something other and new.

Page 158

A child's bedtime prayer. In English the child would say:

I am tired, going to rest.
Father, close my eyes,
And with thine eyes,
Watch over my bed.

The Author

In 1939, at the age of sixteen, **Solomon Stucky** left the Mennonite Church and became a part of a newly formed, local fundamentalist group made up of dissident Mennonites in Kansas.

After graduating from Moundridge High School, he attended a Bible institute in Salina, Kansas, where he met Naomi Kejr, the daughter of a Baptist minister. They were married in 1942. After farming for several years, Sol entered the Baptist ministry.

Over the years his religious philosophy underwent a gradual change. He left the ministry, returned to farming, and eventually both he and his wife received several degrees at Western Michigan University at Kalamazoo.

While a student there in history and religion, Sol met and became friends with Dr. Robert Friedmann, the well-known Anabaptist scholar, who made him very aware of his heritage, not only as an heir of the Anabaptists, but specifically of the unique people known as the Swiss Volhynian Mennonites.

While in graduate school Sol also became involved in the Vietnam situation as a draft counselor, providing assistance to those who chose to go to Canada. Their son was one of the émigrés, and in 1971 the parents followed him and bought a farm east of Toronto. As long as the U.S., draft continued, their large farmhouse was a station on the underground railroad for a number of young war protesters.

Sol feels he has now come full circle in his spiritual pilgrimage, having become again a member in the Mennonite Church in Toronto. He spends most of his time writing. This short novel is about a Swiss Volhynian family and how three generations responded to World War I, World War II, and the Vietnam War. He is the author of *The Heritage of the Swiss Volhynian Mennonites* (Conrad Press, 1981).